A Writer's Commonplace Book

By the Same Author

Fiction
No White Coat
Love on My List
We All Fall Down
Patients of a Saint
The Fraternity
The Commonplace Day
The General Practice
Practice Makes Perfect
The Life Situation
The Long Hot Summer
Proofs of Affection
A Loving Mistress
Rose of Jericho
A Second Wife
To Live in Peace
An Eligible Man
Golden Boy
Vintage
Intensive Care
Paris Summer

Non-fiction
The Writing Game

Juvenile
Aristide
Aristide in Paris

A Writer's Commonplace Book

ROSEMARY FRIEDMAN

MICHAEL O'MARA BOOKS LIMITED

First published in Great Britain in 2006 by
Michael O'Mara Books Limited
9 Lion Yard, Tremadoc Road
London SW4 7NQ

A CIP catalogue record for this book is available
from the British Library

ISBN (10-digit): 1-84317-227-5

ISBN (13-digit): 978-1-84317-227-7

1   3   5   7   9   10   8   6   4   2

www.mombooks.com

Designed and typeset by Martin Bristow

Printed and bound in Great Britain by Clays Ltd, St Ives plc

*For Susan,
Louise, Charlotte
& Emma*

. . . note it in a book, that it may be for the time
to come for ever and ever.

ISAIAH 30:8

A florilegium in which only the string binding
the bouquet of flowers together is mine.

MONTAIGNE

The true pleasure of a commonplace book is the
random nature of its contents.

JOCK MURRAY

Contents

Acknowledgements 8

Foreword 9

On Writers and Writing 11

On Literary Endeavour 50

On Knowledge, Discovery and Travel 96

On Creativity and the Arts 107

On the Human Condition 128

On Love, Marriage and Family 176

On Life and Death 199

On Random Thoughts 220

Index of Contributors 250

Acknowledgements

Thanks are due to my agent, Heather Chalcroft, for her faith in the project; to Susan Close for grappling with my handwriting; to my editor, Helen Cumberbatch, for her patience and hard work; to my husband, Dennis, for his encouragement and support, and to the many authors who provided inspiration for this work and who made it possible.

Foreword

ACCORDING to Pablo Picasso, if one knew exactly what one was going to do there would be not much point in doing it. Little did I think, when I started, many years ago, to keep a record of anything which struck a chord in me during the course of my reading, that one day some of the 3,000 entries in the handwritten volumes would see the light of day.

One of the cardinal rules behind such a compilation is that the moment one comes across a quotation or aphorism one wishes to retain, it must be torn out/copied/memorized/noted immediately. If time is allowed to elapse the publication cannot be recalled, the page number is forgotten and the wise words are lost for ever. For want of a better title, my collection was called *Things* . . . It is a distillation of received wisdom, both from contemporary writers and those who have gone before, on such diverse topics as life and death, books and literature, reading and religion, creativity and travel.

Writing a novel has been compared to setting out alone to cross the Atlantic in a dinghy or having to keep the plans of a cathedral in one's head, and Ralph Waldo Emerson's heart-warming assertion that 'he has not learned the lesson of life who has not every day conquered a new fear', Paul Gauguin's theory that the life of an artist is 'a long road to Calvary', and Jean Sibelius's acid comment that 'no statue has ever been put up to a critic' are reassuring. Often we do not know what we think until we see it written down, and being able to trace an apposite quotation has fuelled my novels, facilitated my research, filled my idle moments, and enriched my life.

Although the sayings in the seven volumes I have to date compiled belong to authors more wise and more eloquent than myself, their silver tongues reflect my views and their often pithy summations confirm my prejudices. *A Writer's Commonplace Book* is an album in which those turning the pages will, I hope, find graphic word-pictures which accurately reflect one writer's thoughts and feelings.

ROSEMARY FRIEDMAN

On Writers and Writing

The writer provides one half and the reader the other.

PAUL VALÉRY

Writers write from a sense of loss.

ANDRÉ GIDE

The difference . . . between the person who says he 'wishes to be a writer' and the person who says he 'wishes to write'. The former desires to be pointed out at cocktail parties, the latter is prepared for the long, solitary hours at a desk; the former desires a status; the latter a process; the former desires to be, the latter to do.

SIR JOHN MORTIMER

All those who live as literary men – working daily as literary labourers – will agree with me that three hours a day will produce as much as a man ought to write.

ANTHONY TROLLOPE

❧

. . . No writer can be a joiner. He must preserve his independence at all costs.

J. B. PRIESTLEY

❧

Every writer is to some extent an outsider to the society in which he lives.

SOURCE UNKNOWN

❧

Writers are a scourge to those they cohabit with. They are present and at the same time they are absent. They are present by the fact of their continuing curiosity, their observing, their cataloguing minds, their longing to see into another person. But the longing is discharged into the work.

EDNA O'BRIEN

❧

Happy productive writers are naturally dull creatures.

CLANCY SEGAL

A writer's obituary should read: 'He wrote books then he died.'

WILLIAM FAULKNER

❧❧

Style is the moment of identity between the writer and his subject.

MARCEL PROUST

❧❧

The true writer doesn't write about the experience he's had but about the experience he's going to have.

T. S. ELIOT

❧❧

A writer knows more than he knows. He has a subconscious ability to read signs.

NADINE GORDIMER

One of the first things you learn as a writer is that you write what you can, not what you want.

GABRIEL GARCÍA MÁRQUEZ

My study, lined with books, reflects my interests, confines my identity as a writer, and reinforces my sense of what kind of person I consider myself to be.

ANTHONY STORR

◈

. . . she [Virginia Woolf] didn't want not to see people, but being continually seen was a pressure.

HERMIONE LEE

◈

. . . a poet and a novelist have about as much in common as a jockey and a diesel driver.

PHILIP ROTH

Technique is not one of the living qualities and the novel is primarily concerned with life. The core quality of the born novelist is human, not literary.

Q. D. LEAVIS

❧

Novelists do not write as birds sing, by the push of nature. It is part of the job that there should be much routine and some daily stuff on the level of carpentry.

WILLIAM GOLDING

❧

Like all obsessive people novelists don't really ask themselves why they do it – so when people ask them they've got to make up reasons.

THOMAS KENEALLY

❧

The poet skims off the best of life and puts it in his work. That is why his work is beautiful and his life bad.

LEO TOLSTOY

❧

Contrary to popular impression, writers, unlike pole vaulters, do not know when they have done their best . . .

JOHN UPDIKE

The readers' feelings are stirred only when the author's own are engaged, and an author will then score a bestseller when his hopes, fears and prejudices coincide with those of the many. That is less likely if he has a literary background to distance him from his clientèle.

SOURCE UNKNOWN

❧

As a matter of fact in all my writing I tell the story of my life ... Only the dilettantes try to be universal; a real writer knows that he's connected with a certain people or a certain time, a certain environment and there he stays.

ISAAC BASHEVIS SINGER

❧

God keep me from ever completing anything. This whole book is but a draft – nay, but the draft of a draft. Oh. Time, Strength, Cash and Patience!

HERMAN MELVILLE

❧

For those who put pen to paper do so because they rarely trust their own voices, and indeed, in society, have very little to say. They are, as I now know, the least entertaining of guests.

ANITA BROOKNER

. . . writers and dancers had the most difficulty learning to talk in public, because each had chosen a profession in which they could communicate without speech.

GLORIA STEINEM

❧

You can't decide to become a writer as you might become a doctor or a plumber. Long before you have a conscious choice, it has been made for you.

JOHN FOWLES

❧

Novelists . . . had been reduced to the role of occasional entertainers, pushed off the front page by pop stars, tennis players and seedy politicians.

SOURCE UNKNOWN

A true classic, as I should like to hear it defined, is an author who has enriched the human mind, increased its treasure and caused it to advance a step.

SAINTE-BEUVE

❧

Self-employed writers are paid 'per word, per piece or perhaps'.

ROBERT BENCHLEY

❧

Nothing can injure a man's writing if he's a first-rate writer.

WILLIAM FAULKNER

❧

The function of a writer is to raise questions not to find answers.

DORIS LESSING

. . . she [Virginia Woolf] couldn't reread her own books, she would 'shudder past them on the shelf as if they might bite me'.

HERMIONE LEE

❧

Writers and artists have their own slide rule in their belly.

NORMAN LEAR

❧

A writer is someone who sits full-time at his desk, earns his bread by writing, is concerned with problems of style and language, and aspires to recognition.

PRIMO LEVI

❧

The most essential gift for a good writer is a built-in, shock-proof shit detector. This is the writer's radar and all great writers have had it.

ERNEST HEMINGWAY

❧

Most writers write to say something about other people – and it doesn't last. Good writers write to find out about themselves – and it lasts forever.

GLORIA STEINEM

Writing is not a profession, but a vocation of unhappiness.
I don't think an artist can ever be happy.

GEORGES SIMENON

❧

Mrs Gaskell said she wrote in a room with six doors, thus
enabling her innumerable children to interrupt her freely,
while through further doors came requests for dinner
menus and plans for the day.

SOURCE UNKNOWN

❧

Isadora's desk appeared a random mess, but like a novel in
progress it had an inner logic apparent only to its begetter.

ERICA JONG

❧

. . . to describe a novelist as a mere story-teller is to dismiss
him with contumely.

W. SOMERSET MAUGHAM

❧

I hate everything that does not relate to literature.
Conversations bore me . . . to visit people bores me, the
sorrows and joys of my relatives bore me to my soul.

FRANZ KAFKA

On Writers and Writing

... a writer is someone born with a gift. An athlete can run. A painter can paint. A writer has a facility with words. A good writer can also think. Isn't that enough to define a writer by?

CYNTHIA OZICK

❧

... I never show my own MSS to anyone; and only let them read them when they're hard and fast finished.

VIRGINIA WOOLF

❧

I can't understand writers who feel they shouldn't have to do any of the ordinary things of life, because I think that this is necessary; one has got to keep in touch with that.

NADINE GORDIMER

. . . every writer of fiction, though he may not adopt the dramatic form, writes in effect for the stage.

CHARLES DICKENS

❦

Being an author is not a profession it's a condition.

JOHN WAIN

❦

When I am dead, I hope it may be said:
'His sins were scarlet, but his books were read.'

HILAIRE BELLOC

❦

'How can I become a writer?'
'You can't.'
'But you did.'
'I didn't have to ask.'

SOURCE UNKNOWN

❦

All writers arrange objects around them in a way that means nothing to anyone except their owner. Then you feel safe and can set out on some sort of voyage of the mind knowing you're going to find your way back.

REDMOND O'HANLON

It can be argued that no writer had a clearer insight than Shakespeare, and he managed to achieve this in a world without refrigeration, Darwin, Freud, Bill Gates, emails, television or the mobile phone.

SIR JOHN MORTIMER

❧

A good novelist does not have to describe everything about the sea as long as he knows it.

ERNEST HEMINGWAY

❧

George Bernard Shaw insisted that he would start at the top of the page without the slightest inkling of what was going to happen by the bottom of it.

DAVID CAMPTON

No man but a blockhead ever wrote except for money.

SAMUEL JOHNSON

❧

If I had listened to what people said I would never have been a writer.

JOHN WAIN

❧

I think I am a bit schizoid: there is the person that is me and the person who writes.

WILLIAM TREVOR

❧

. . . writers have no game plan. 'You write what you enjoy.'

TOM STOPPARD

❧

Orwell said that, like all writers, he was 'driven on by some demon whom one can neither resist nor understand.'

JACK HODGES

❧

. . . authors are, in the main, abysmally treated by their publishers.

DAVID ELLIOT

He [Dickens] still needed a name to begin. On a sheet of paper he transcribed all the titles of his previous novels, and then wrote Martin Chizzlewig, then M Chubblewig, then Cluzzletoe and Cluzzlebog . . . 'I shall never be able to do anything for the work until it has a fixed name.'

PETER ACKROYD

. . . when one thinks of Balzac, Tolstoy and Dickens I don't think any contemporary novelist can claim to be of that stature . . . The greatness of each man lies in the depth of characterization, then skill in narrative and their kind of universal appeal.

GRAHAM GREENE

❧

. . . writers are supposed to make you laugh and cry. That's what mankind is looking for.

SAUL BELLOW

I tell myself what I have always told myself. It is what all writers have told themselves, consciously or otherwise. The things you feel are universal.

MARTIN AMIS

๑✦๑

Authors frequently conceal their natural (and cultivated) envy, spite and malice behind public displays of affability and mutual praise.

JULIAN BARNES

๑✦๑

I think like a genius, write like an accomplished author and talk like a child.

VLADIMIR NABOKOV

๑✦๑

Most classic playwrights seem to have been born knowing all about keeping an audience interested. I doubt if Shakespeare or Shaw read a book on how to do it in their lives.

DAVID CAMPTON

๑✦๑

Dickens evidently works upon no plan; he has a leading idea, but no design at all.

PETER ACKROYD

Some writers will not set out unless they have the most exact route maps.

SOURCE UNKNOWN

❧

Nervy, insecure and self-absorbed, first-rate writers are all too rarely first-rate people.

FRANCIS KING

❧

Who can measure the ecstasy that Homer inspired, or count the tears that the excellent Horace has changed into smiles?

GUSTAVE FLAUBERT

❧

A man may write at any time, if he will set himself doggedly to do it.

SAMUEL JOHNSON

He [Arthur Koestler] needs absolute solitude, so I work two floors below. He minds terribly if he is interrupted, so I don't go up and tell him lunch is ready. Instead I buzz him. I stay well out of range.

CYNTHIA KOESTLER

❧

No one wants a midlist. An author is either on the way up, or on the way out.

HELEN FRASER

❧

It seems to me that Auden was much nearer to describing the novelist's craft when he wrote of suffering, how it takes place when someone else is eating or opening a window or just walking dully along.

PHILIP LARKIN

❧

. . . there is nothing so pleasurable for a man as to have produced a play that delights the town.

SAMUEL JOHNSON

❧

The creator is nothing, the work everything.

GUSTAVE FLAUBERT

When you get down to it, what an audience wants to hear from a novelist is how he writes.

WILLIAM GOLDING

❧

All my characters are galley slaves and I am the man on the deck with the whip.

VLADIMIR NABOKOV

❧

. . . it is a very obvious truth that the deepest quality of a work of art will always be the mind of the producer . . . No good novel ever proceeded from a superficial mind.

HENRY JAMES

The business of the poet and the novelist is to show the sorriness underlying the grandest things, and the grandeur underlying the sorriest things.

THOMAS HARDY

❧

All writers draw heavily on 'the compost of the mind'.

MARTHA GELLHORN

... he [the writer] is a secreter of images, some of which he prays will have the immortal resistance of Don Quixote's windmills, or Proust's Madeleine, of Huck Finn's raft.

JOHN UPDIKE

❧

No one incapable of restraint was ever a writer ...

SOURCE UNKNOWN

Not another of these interminable novels exposing the shallowness of everything except the author.

VINCENT BROME

❧

If to understand someone's writing you have to tear a paragraph apart and wrestle with it on the carpet, then the novelist is not doing his job.

ERIC LINKLATER

❧

. . . Shakespeare's unique ability to understand the human soul and its needs and powers, and to clothe that understanding in thoughts and words . . .

BERNARD LEVIN

❧

For the novelist, choosing a title may be an important part of the creative process, bringing into sharper focus what the novel is supposed to be about.

DAVID LODGE

❧

Like the Russians he [D. H. Lawrence] made the days of his characters' lives more important than the plot.

V. S. PRITCHETT

Sometimes, when I am empty, when words won't come,
when I find I haven't written a single sentence after scribbling
whole pages, I collapse on my couch and lie there dazed,
bogged in a swamp of despair, hating myself and blaming
myself . . . A quarter of an hour later, everything has changed;
my heart is pounding with joy.

GUSTAVE FLAUBERT

❧

Writers that hang out together are no bloody good.

ERNEST HEMINGWAY

❧

. . . the genuine artist writes what he has to, and if it is what
he *really* has to then he will be able to persuade us. That is
why talk about the death of the novel is such nonsense.

GABRIEL JOSIPOVICI

❧

. . . his [the novelist's] greatness is in direct proportion to the
width and depth of his vision. His window has to be filled
with an all-embracing view, even if his subject is only a
garden with a girl in it. His ears have to be filled with the
harmonies and discords of the great symphony, even if his
attention is concentrated on the voice of a simple flute.

CECIL DAY LEWIS

There's nothing more wearing than having to go around pretending to be the author of one's own books — except pretending not to be.

PHILIP ROTH

❧

It is true that the first rule for a writer is to hold his audience . . . it must not be forgotten that John Buchan and Agatha Christie knew it as well as Dostoyevsky and Kafka.

GABRIEL JOSIPOVICI

What point of morals, of manners, of economy, of philosophy, or religion, of taste, of the conduct of life, has he [Shakespeare] not settled? What mystery has he not signified his knowledge of? What office, or function, or district of man's work, has he not remembered?

RALPH WALDO EMERSON

. . . a writer who knows his craft can say all he wishes to say without affronting the good manners or infringing the conventions of his time.

GEORGE STEINER

❧

. . . we [writers] are not a symphony but a mob of one-man bands, one-person bands I should say, playing all simultaneously, and mostly unheard.

JOHN UPDIKE

Balzac recognized that a desire satisfied may mean a work not created. 'A woman one sleeps with is a novel one does not write.'

JEAN GIMPEL

On Writers and Writing

I write for the sake of the pleasure it gives me, and for the difficulty. I like composing riddles and finding elegant solutions.

VLADIMIR NABOKOV

❧

. . . writers only write well when they listen to what they are writing – either on magnetic tape or in the auditorium set silently in their skulls.

ANTHONY BURGESS

❧

I know the value of publicity, I am not opposed to it, but for a man of letters modesty and an attitude towards readers and fellow writers that suits literature is the best and most effective publicity.

ANTON CHEKHOV

❧

Last week I spent *five days writing one page* . . .

GUSTAVE FLAUBERT

❧

. . . full time, which for a writer is three or four hours of creative composition a day . . .

ANTHONY BLOND

Nothing really frightens me but the idea of forced idleness. As long as I can write books, even though they be not published, I think that I can be happy.

ANTHONY TROLLOPE

Every true novelist listens for that suprapersonal wisdom, which explains why great novels are always a little more intelligent than their authors. Novelists who are more intelligent than their works should change profession.

MILAN KUNDERA

Chaucer lives in Spenser, who lives in Dryden who lives in Keats.

GEORGE STEINER

Plot comes of course from character, but as E. M. Forster has pointed out, you may create the most scintillating characters who will sit about and be too lazy to involve themselves in a plot at all.

SIR JOHN MORTIMER

❧

Those who write (unlike those who do) have the luxury of being against all establishments.

JOHN FOWLES

❧

. . . if you write for long enough and often enough, it becomes in the end as natural a function as breathing or eating . . .

FAY WELDON

❧

He [Ivan Turgenev] always understood how to insert points of rest in which a story can grow of itself.

SOURCE UNKNOWN

❧

Why does the writing make us chase the writer? Why can't we leave well enough alone? Why aren't the books enough?

JULIAN BARNES

Writers need solitude as others need sleep.

SOURCE UNKNOWN

❧

I write fifty pages until I hear a foetal heartbeat.

HENRY MILLER

❧

Unless one is a moron, one always dies unsure of one's own value and that of one's works. Virgil himself, as he lay dying, wanted the Aeneid burned.

GUSTAVE FLAUBERT

❧

It is by sitting down to write every morning that one becomes a writer. Those who do not do this remain amateur.

GERALD BRENAN

❧

I write when I'm inspired and I see to it that I'm inspired at 9 o'clock every morning.

PETER DE VRIES

❧

. . . we are lucky people, our work is amusement.

LEO TOLSTOY

He [Flaubert] despised publicity and scorned those writers who put their photographs on their books.

JULIAN BARNES

He [Dickens] discovered . . . the formula 'laughter and tears' that has been the foundation of practically every popular success ever since (Hollywood's as well as the bestseller's).

Q. D. LEAVIS

. . . he [Anthony Trollope] began a 'commonplace book', which went into two volumes, in which he made notes about authors and their books . . .

VICTORIA GLENDINNING

You once said that you would like to sit beside me while I write. Listen, in that case I could not write at all . . . one can never be alone enough when one writes, why there can never be enough silence around one when one is writing, why even night is not night enough.

FRANZ KAFKA

Most authors understand no more about literature than birds do about ornithology.

MARCEL REICH-RANICKI

I don't think it's possible to write anything good unless it's autobiographical.

DAVID MAMET

If you steal from one book you are condemned as a plagiarist, but if you steal from ten books you are considered a scholar, and if steal from thirty or forty books, a distinguished scholar.

AMOS OZ

I don't invent it — really do not — *but* see it, and write it down.

CHARLES DICKENS

The point is, as Aristotle told us, is what happens to the *hero* . . . not what happens to the writer.

DAVID MAMET

. . . an extreme negative emotion held against other human beings for reasons they do not control can be blinding. Blindness about other human beings, especially for a writer is equivalent to death.

ALICE WALKER

Many people believe they have a novel in them; few get to write one, fewer still to see it published.

SOURCE UNKNOWN

. . . what boring company novelists are because they're always half-listening to the next conversation and half-thinking about their own work.

V. S. PRITCHETT

. . . it is his [Dickens'] ability to recognize and refine human feeling which makes him so great a novelist.

PETER ACKROYD

It's only after you've written a book that you find out what it's about because everyone tells you.

HELEN FIELDING

A writer's life truly does depend on his desk, and if he wants to avoid madness, he mustn't strictly speaking, ever leave his desk, he must cling to it with gritted teeth.

SOURCE UNKNOWN

I do not boast about the quality of my work, but I may be permitted to pride myself on the gift of steady application.

ANTHONY BURGESS

I like idling when I ought not to be idling . . . The time when I like best to stand with my back to the fire . . . is when my desk is heaped highest with letters that must be answered by the next post . . . if for some urgent reason, I ought to be up particularly early in the morning, it is then . . . that I love to lie an extra half hour in bed.

JEROME K. JEROME

❧

. . . a writer is, by definition, one who is most alive when alone. But there's a big bill to pay. It makes you very detached.

MARTIN AMIS

❧

. . . the conversation of an American writer is no different from that of a realtor – money and the storms of domestic life. What little reading most writers do tends to be of a competitive nature. Who has written what, and why it has failed or, worse, succeeded.

GORE VIDAL

❧

Writing itself is an important freedom: 'in writing I feel I have some control over the world; I can recreate the world a little bit more to my own liking.'

GRACE NICHOLS

What I gained from Joyce was this awed realization that you don't have to go anywhere at all except round the corner to flesh out a literary work.

HENRY ROTH

❧

A problem with writing the life of a writer is that writers don't have a life.

JASPER GERARD

❧

The pain that secretly or openly gnaws at a man attracts the Russian writer.

ANATOLY VARMAN

❧

His [Charles Dickens'] daughter once observed that, when he was writing his fiction, he would literally act out the words in front of a mirror before placing them down on paper . . .

PETER ACKROYD

❧

If you are a writer, by definition it seems to me you're pretty neurotic. And the whole writing business is some way of coming to terms with it.

DORIS LESSING

And given the hours put in, the money isn't all that good. Counting taxation and time spent, most writers make less than dental hygienists.

ERICA JONG

. . . the stronger the writer the stronger the suffering . . .

HAROLD BLOOM

You shouldn't show your writings to anyone before they are published. You'll hear more harmful opinions than good advice.

LEO TOLSTOY

I hear, as do we all, of these people who spend eight to ten hours a day at their typewriters, and I think, has no one told them of the Nap?

DAVID MAMET

My stories come to me and ask to be written. They come without asking at all sorts of strange times. But if I don't write them down they go away.

ALISON UTTLEY

She [Mrs Trollope] got up to write at four in the morning and her stint was done before the family woke up.

VICTORIA GLENDINNING

❧

Characters have to *yearn* for something, not just to fall in love.

SYDNEY POLLACK

❧

Great novelists must make use of their lives and those of other people on their own terms.

JOHN BAYLEY

On Writers and Writing

I am not aware of other styles of writing. I do my own. I write in my own way. I have no models.

V. S. NAIPAUL

❦

Most authors are paid a pittance in return for the time it takes to produce finely crafted books.

GILES GORDON

❦

The mark of a good writer is one who can hold two opposing opinions in his head at the same time.

SOURCE UNKNOWN

❦

Of course you're a writer, you need to meet all kinds of people . . . that's only natural for a man in your position. People from the sports' world, from the movies, musicians, commodity brokers, criminals too. They're your bread and butter, meat and potatoes.

SAUL BELLOW

❦

. . . what Marcel [Proust] most liked reading before going to sleep was a train timetable.

ALAIN DE BOTTON

Let no one say that I have said nothing new; the arrangement of the subject is new.

BLAISE PASCAL

... I carry chair, writing materials, rug and cushion into the garden, but am called in to have a look at the Pantry Sink, please, as it seems to have blocked itself up. Attempted return to garden frustrated by arrival of note from the village concerning Garden Fête ... necessity for speaking to butcher on the telephone and sudden realization that Laundry List hasn't yet been made out, and the van will be here at eleven.

E. M. DELAFIELD

The best research is talking to people.

JEFFREY ARCHER

A proper writer refines and edits: the first creative flush may happen as quickly as the writing of a hasty letter or scribbling of a note. After that comes the real work of going back and back again to the words on the page to make sure that they convey exactly what is intended; or as nearly as possible.

SOURCE UNKNOWN

❧

Novels by serious writers of genius often eventually become bestsellers, but most contemporary bestsellers are written by second-class writers whose psychological brew contains a touch of naivety, a touch of sentimentality, the storytelling gift of a mysterious sympathy with the daydreams of ordinary people.

LEONARD WOOLF

❧

You can. You know you can conquer your fears. That's what a writer is — a conqueror of fears.

ERICA JONG

❧

I sometimes think it is because they are so bad at expressing themselves verbally that writers take to pen and paper in the first place.

GORE VIDAL

On Literary Endeavour

To write well, express yourself like the common people, but think like a wise man.

ARISTOTLE

❧

Each word should be weighed carefully as for a telegram to be paid for by the author.

ERNEST HEMINGWAY

❧

The more you write the nicer you become.

VIRGINIA WOOLF

❧

Drama thrives on conflict, and so does the novel.

ARTHUR KOESTLER

❧

Write what you know around you, make use of the soil beneath your feet, of the tradition within your heart, of the struggle in your soul, of the breath in your hills.

F. H. KOCH

The art of writing is a very futile business if it does not imply first of all the art of seeing the world as the potentiality of fiction.

VLADIMIR NABOKOV

❧

Writing is always creating order from disorder. Order is something that needs disorder to take form. The only order one can trust is the order of the mind, internal order. And nothing is more disordered than a human mind.

ITALO CALVINO

Originality is nothing but judicious plagiarism . . .

VOLTAIRE

❧

He [Shakespeare] was not a man, he was a continent; he contained whole crowds of great men, entire landscapes.

GUSTAVE FLAUBERT

And to this moment a day when I have produced nothing printable, when I have not gotten any words out, is a day lost and damned as I feel it.

JOHN UPDIKE

❧

... literature deals mostly with the characters of people — their feelings, their way of talking, and behaviour in various circumstances.

ISAAC BASHEVIS SINGER

❧

Rule one is quite simple: 'Have one hand holding your pen and the other firmly in the nape of the readers neck.'

WILLIAM GOLDING

The creative act was like being given an undeveloped film. 'All I had to do was develop it.'

VLADIMIR NABOKOV

Reading a work of art in translation is like making love through a blanket.

AMOS OZ

❦

There are too many books published. It is one of the evils of democracy.

T. S. ELIOT

❦

Bad novels are not bad because their characters do not live, but because 'they do not live with one another', only through the author.

SOURCE UNKNOWN

❦

. . . The proper stuff of fiction does not exist. Everything is the proper stuff of fiction, every feeling, every thought; every quality of brain and spirit is drawn upon; no perception comes amiss.

VIRGINIA WOOLF

❦

A good prose sentence should be like a good line of poetry – unchangeable, just as rhythmic, just as sonorous.

GUSTAVE FLAUBERT

Writing is a form of therapy; sometimes I wonder how all those who do not write, compose or paint can manage to escape the madness, the melancholia, the panic and fear which is inherent in the human situation.

GRAHAM GREENE

❧

Auschwitz defies the novelist's language, the historian's analysis, the vision of the prophet.

ELIE WIESEL

❧

. . . in all my years browsing around Charing Cross Road I've almost never seen anyone . . . buying the kind of book that gets reviewed.

DAVID CAUTE

❧

Of making many books there is no end.

ECCLESIASTES 12:12

❧

Great novels begin with the tiny hints – the sliver of Madeleine melting in Proust's mouth, the shade of louse-gray that Flaubert had in mind for Madame Bovary.

JOHN UPDIKE

Paperbacks do *not* make for the collection of a library.

GEORGE STEINER

❦

The world craves book reviews far more heartily than it craves books . . .

JOHN UPDIKE

❦

Fiction is telling Lies.

SOURCE UNKNOWN

❦

. . . the novel gives the longest surcease from ennui at the least expenditure of time and money.

Q. D. LEAVIS

In very large measure, most books are about previous books.

GEORGE STEINER

❧

Everything comes out of silence. If you're silent for a long time people just appear in your mind.

GLORIA STEINEM

❧

To write about love and exclude sex was a useless labour.

ISAAC BASHEVIS SINGER

❧

The whole idea of arranging literature in a hierarchical order is one that is completely contrary to the literary idea.

SIMONE DE BEAUVOIR

❧

. . . modern softening of these traditional psychodramas (fairy tales) prevents them from doing their work; the violence already exists within the child and must be spoken to.

BRUNO BETTELHEIM

❧

Get black on white.

GUY DE MAUPASSANT

On Literary Endeavour

To do a piece [a review] well takes a long time, and time is not a thing that I am eager to fling idly through life's transom window.

GORE VIDAL

⛦

Literature flourishes best when it is half a trade and half an art.

WILLIAM RALPH INGE

⛦

The difference between literature and journalism is that journalism is unreadable and literature is not read.

OSCAR WILDE

⛦

Language is like a cracked kettle on which we beat out tunes for bears to dance to, while all the time we long to move the stars to pity.

GUSTAVE FLAUBERT

⛦

For our world of books, like most other worlds now, is the arena of an increasingly bitter struggle for space – for paper and cover cloth, for review space, and for the limited reading time that a busy citizen in this electronic age can afford.

JOHN UPDIKE

It [the novel] must take itself seriously for the public to take it so.

HENRY JAMES

❧

'Oh! It is only a novel!' . . . or, in short, only some work in which the greatest powers of the mind are displayed, in which the most thorough knowledge of human nature, the happiest delineation of its varieties, the liveliest effusions of wit and humour, are conveyed to the world in the best-chosen language.

JANE AUSTEN

I do with my friends as I do with my books, I would have them where I can find them, but seldom use them.

RALPH WALDO EMERSON

❧

Genuine Literature informs while it entertains.

ISAAC BASHEVIS SINGER

On Literary Endeavour

Literature: writings in verse or prose of acknowledged excellence whose value lies in their intense, personal expression of life.

Source unknown

❧

One does not choose one's subject matter, one submits to it.

Gustave Flaubert

❧

The truth is that, by writing about them, 'agonies' are mitigated: literature exorcises them or makes them endurable.

Mario Vargas Llosa

❧

I wrote the sort of piece I should like to go to a theatre to see; one in which people say and do things that make me laugh.

Gore Vidal

❧

I leave the myth of inspiration and agonized creative inaction to the amateurs. The practice of a profession entails discipline, which for me meant the production of two thousand words of fair copy every day, weekends included.

Anthony Burgess

Some books are to be tasted, others to be swallowed, and some few to be chewed and digested.

FRANCIS BACON

❧

This is not a novel to be tossed side lightly, it should be thrown with great force.

DOROTHY PARKER

❧

Another damned thick square book. Always scribble, scribble, scribble, eh, Mr Gibbon?

WILLIAM HENRY, DUKE OF GLOUCESTER

❧

. . . a good talker can talk away the substance of twenty books in as many evenings. He will describe the central idea of a book he means to write until it revolts him.

W. SOMERSET MAUGHAM

❧

You should go to your room every day at nine o'clock . . . and say to yourself, 'I am going to sit here for four hours and write!' . . . if you sit waiting for inspiration, you will sit there till you are an old man.

SIR WINSTON CHURCHILL

On Literary Endeavour

L'auteur, dans son oeuvre, doit être comme Dieu dans l'univers, present partout, et visible nulle part.

GUSTAVE FLAUBERT

❧

Only connect the prose and the passion, and both will be exalted.

E. M. FORSTER

❧

Literature is mostly about having sex and not much about having children. Life is the other way round.

DAVID LODGE

❧

Today publishers are reluctant to publish first novels by anyone who has not been at the very least, a movie star or serial killer.

GORE VIDAL

The only thing worth writing about is the conflict in the human heart.

WILLIAM FAULKNER

❧

. . . André Gide turned down for Editions Gallimard, *Swann's Way* . . . James Joyce's *Ulysses* had to be privately printed in France . . . *Dubliners* went unpublished for ten years . . .

FRANCIS WHEEN

. . . the business of recording life meant that there was less time for living.

DORIS LESSING

❧

A boy's gotta hustle his book.

TRUMAN CAPOTE

❧

Novels are made out of people.

ANTHONY BURGESS

Even a child knows that if they (publishers) don't spend money on it they're not going to sell it.

MARTIN AMIS

❧

Fiction is nothing less than the subtlest instrument for self-examination or self display that mankind has invented yet.

JOHN UPDIKE

❧

When you write, 'tell a story' and don't try to explain the story. If you say that a boy fell in love with a girl, you don't have to explain to the reader why a boy falls in love. The reader knows as much as you – or more, so you 'tell him the story' and the explanations and interpretations he will make for himself!

ISAAC BASHEVIS SINGER

❧

One ancient test for the novel remains fiercely valid: unless it demands rereading, the work does not qualify.

HAROLD BLOOM

❧

Childhood is a writer's bank balance.

GRAHAM GREENE

His [Shakespeare's] mind is the horizon, beyond which, at present, we do not see.

RALPH WALDO EMERSON

◈

People talked about his [Dickens'] characters as if they were next-door neighbours or friends.

GEORGE ELIOT

◈

Of all the needs a book has, the chief need is that it be readable.

ANTHONY TROLLOPE

◈

When *A Hundred Years of Solitude* (Márquez) came out, it got no good reviews at all. Roll on three or four years and it becomes an unquestioned classic!

DORIS LESSING

◈

. . . the question that works with all other playwrights and novelists — with which character do we identify? — simply makes no sense with Shakespeare, whose genius ensures that we are Iago as well as Othello, Hamlet and Claudius, Lear and his daughters, Montagues and Capulets.

BERNARD LEVIN

I am aware that these little books don't last long, even if they are a success.

BEATRIX POTTER

❧

Generally, in literature, goodness has always been bad news . . . happiness 'writes white'.

MARTIN AMIS

❧

If you want to say that it is raining, say 'It is raining.'

LA BRUYÈRE

❧

Drama is not suited to the analysis of character, which is the province of the novel. Dramatic characters are simplified, easily recognizable and over life-size.

W. H. AUDEN

Thank you for sending me a copy of your book. I'll waste no time in reading it.

SOURCE UNKNOWN

❧

Imagination is everything. Knowing is nothing.

ANATOLE FRANCE

❧

One resents being axed from the narrative apart from anything else. I'd have liked to know the outcome.

PENELOPE LIVELY

❧

... Save your priapism for style, fuck your inkwell ...

GUSTAVE FLAUBERT

❧

Unless you catch ideas on the wing and nail them down, you will soon cease to have any.

VIRGINIA WOOLF

❧

If it reads easy, it was writ hard.

ERNEST HEMINGWAY

On Literary Endeavour

The only safe way of deciding whether a novel is good or bad is simply to observe one's own sensations on reading the last page.

VIRGINIA WOOLF

Good prose is like a window pane. Concentrate on sharpening your memory and peeling your sensibility. Cut every page you write by at least a third. Stop constructing these piddling little similes of yours. Work out what you want to say. Then say it in the most direct and vigorous way you can.

GEORGE ORWELL

❧

Thoughts come clearly when one walks.

THOMAS MANN

. . . I'm not a teacher. I couldn't be. I should think that chewing over other people's work, writing I mean, must be terribly stultifying. Quite sicken you with the whole business of literature . . . It would be death to me to have to think about literature as such, to say why one poem was 'better' than another and so on.

PHILIP LARKIN

❦

Fine sentiments make bad literature.

ANDRÉ GIDE

❦

Comedy and tragedy — like a piece of streaky bacon.

CHARLES DICKENS

❦

I never read a book before I review it; it prejudices a man so.

REV. SYDNEY SMITH

❦

I think about the literary world like I think about Tibet. It's quite interesting. It's a long way away from me, and it's sure as hell that they're never going to make me Dalai Lama.

TERRY PRATCHETT

On Literary Endeavour

In real life people do not spend every minute shooting each other, hanging themselves or making declarations of love. They don't spend every minute saying clever things. Rather they eat, drink, flirt, talk nonsense. And that is what should be seen on stage.

ANTON CHEKHOV

You'd be amazed how much you find you know when you start writing.

SOURCE UNKNOWN

A play is not about nice things happening to nice people. A play is about rather terrible things happening to people who are as nice or not nice as we ourselves are.

DAVID MAMET

The best place to write is in your head.

ERNEST HEMINGWAY

๛

The only way is to go up a mountain and write.

PHILIP ROTH

๛

In the end all drama is about family.

JOYCE CAROL OATES

๛

Kakfa never won a prize. James Joyce never won a prize . . . We are fashioning a world where excellence and prize winning are seen as synonymous. And they are not.

CARLO GEBLER

๛

We don't want literature, my friend: we want a bestseller.

ANTHONY BURGESS

๛

I decided that I'd probably lose my interest in literature if I were to study it. I like putting books down when they bore me. I think that's a fundamental right that a reader has . . .

VIKRAM SETH

I am dying and the whore Emma Bovary will live for ever.

GUSTAVE FLAUBERT

❧

I hold my inventive capacity on the stern condition that it must master my whole life, often have complete possession of me, make its own demands upon me, and sometimes for months together put everything else away for me.

CHARLES DICKENS

❧

It is remarkable that the most imaginative erotic episode in French literature does not contain a single allusion to the female body or a single word of love . . .

MARIO VARGAS LLOSA

❧

Wherever they burn books they will also, in the end, burn human beings.

HEINRICH HEINE

My task is to chronicle these little daily lacerations upon the spirit.

ANTHONY TROLLOPE

❧

If your writing isn't working, the reader will go into the kitchen and make a cheese sandwich and never come back.

ALISTAIR MACLEOD

❧

Everything in life is an experience for an artist — so nothing is thrown away.

JOHN MASEFIELD

❧

Short Story — The art at a glance.

WILLIAM TREVOR

❧

Write it down or it's lost.

CHRISTOPHER ISHERWOOD

❧

To write fiction is to learn to inhabit other skins, whether thinner or thicker than one's own.

GRAHAM GREENE

On Literary Endeavour

It is not necessary to treat rare books like china. There are only two rules. Wash your hands first and put the books away afterwards.

JEANETTE WINTERSON

A memoir is how one remembers one's own life. An autobiography is history.

GORE VIDAL

Writing a book is a horrible, exhausting struggle, like a long bout of some painful illness.

GEORGE ORWELL

Talking about a novel in progress is like opening the oven door on a soufflé.

NIGEL NICOLSON

It [writing] is oddly enough a physical as well as a mental satisfaction. I like to feel the process of composition in my brain . . . one of the most unfailing pleasures is to sit down in the morning and write.

LEONARD WOOLF

❧

Characters without contradictions are like eggs without salt.

SIR JOHN MORTIMER

❧

Of course I draw from life, but I always pulp my acquaintance before serving them up. You would never recognize a pig in a sausage.

MRS TROLLOPE

On Literary Endeavour

When you're writing, a kind of instinct comes into play.
What you're going to write is already there in the darkness
... it's a matter of deciphering something already there,
something you've already done in the course of your life, in
its organic rumination, unbeknown to you.

MARGUERITE DURAS

❧

Writing a novel does not become easier with practice.

GRAHAM GREENE

❧

It is a delicious thing to write, whether well or badly, to be
no longer yourself but to move in an entire universe of your
own creation.

GUSTAVE FLAUBERT

❧

... sentimentality causes us not merely to write in clichés
but to think in clichés ...

ROGER SCRUTON

❧

If you are writing a book, make sure that the beginning is
really good ...

STUART SUTHERLAND

That's how God arranged it — that those who know life can't write, while those blessed with talent are dreamers who only know their own fantasies.

ISAAC BASHEVIS SINGER

❧

What one wants from writing is habit.

VIRGINIA WOOLF

❧

You write in order to say the things you can't say. It's a cry, or a scream or a song.

SAMUEL BECKETT

❧

There is no need to find a story. Simply men in their context of life, in their own atmosphere. Then the little push of the finger that sets them going . . .

GEORGES SIMENON

❧

Do not imagine you can exorcise what oppresses you in life by giving vent to it in art. No. The heart's dross does not find its way onto paper: all you pour out there is ink.

GUSTAVE FLAUBERT

On Literary Endeavour

As we read *War and Peace*, 'great chords begin to sound'. It is as majestic and as moving in its grandeur and immensity as Beethoven's Fifth Symphony.

E. M. FORSTER

❧

Always carry a pencil and paper.

ROBERT HARDY

❧

. . . I worked with a pencil, and what I wrote my wife copied afterwards.

ANTHONY TROLLOPE

The central emotion of a short story should be austere, major. The subject must have implicit dignity.

ELIZABETH BOWEN

Tell the story, take out the good lines, and see if it still works.

ERNEST HEMINGWAY

❧

. . . the subject of literature is the relation of human beings to each other.

SUSAN SONTAG

❧

The only justification for a book's existence is that it absorbs you, fully and without compromise.

SAUL BELLOW

❧

The history of a flea can be as fine as the story of Alexander the Great: everything depends on the execution.

GUSTAVE FLAUBERT

❧

Writing is a hopeless attempt to heal the festering disease of the soul.

ANTHONY BURGESS

❧

Even the finest books deserve to be thrown aside.

ALAIN DE BOTTON

. . . you will find that people who lack elementary culture keep books not as tools of learning but as decoration for their dining-rooms. So we should buy enough books for use, and none just for embellishment.

SENECA

People ask if I have myself read all the books I quote. I reply that I have not . . .

BLAISE PASCAL

'What is the use of a book,' thought Alice, 'without pictures or conversations?'

LEWIS CARROLL

'For Sale. Baby's Shoes. Never Worn.'

ERNEST HEMINGWAY
(*Story in half a dozen words*)

His [Plato's] complaint against books was that when one tried to question them they remained silent and that if one sought to attack them they did not reply.

Jean Gimpel

❦

It is only if you have a definite person in your mind that you can give vitality and authenticity to your own creation.

Ivan Turgenev

❦

If you steal from one author, it's plagiarism; if you steal from many it's research.

Wilson Mizner

❦

. . . almost every book that has ever attracted great numbers of readers, has provided concrete information, not only expressions of emotion or moral intent.

C. P. Snow

On Literary Endeavour

The whole process of composition is of straining to catch and record something of harmony and sense as it is relayed from an unknown source and gradually forms itself into words . . . The final stage in a painful process of *listening to oneself* in a search for the objective and absolute precise unity called a 'poem'.

NADEZHDA MANDELSTAM

To me the first thing to know before starting a novel is the characters. I accept as a rule that a novel based on an idea or a plot is almost by definition a bad novel . . . if the characters are true the plot will come easily.

GEORGES SIMENON

Writing, after all, is part of life, an overflow of it. Take away life and you take away writing.

FAY WELDON

The 'what have we here' approach will yield a reviewer fruitful results . . . the book ought to be well-written. It should tell me a story without rushing through it with the characters well drawn.

SANDRA COHEN

Far too many relied on the classic formula of a beginning, a middle, and an end.

PHILIP LARKIN

❦

. . . the great ones [books] are those that one enjoys and the enjoyment does not fade.

DAVID HOLLOWAY

❦

The aim of literature was to write a book that would reveal to the reader things he had never thought of before.

SIMONE DE BEAUVOIR

❦

Above all, don't write literature.

COLETTE

... We have histories of books, of paper, of inks and typography, but none of reading.

GEORGE STEINER

❧

Books are the true levellers. They give to all who faithfully use them the society and the spiritual presence of the best and greatest of our race.

WILLIAM ELLERY CHANNING

❧

Fiction stretches our sensibilities and our understanding as mere information never can.

FAY WELDON

❧

I've always found it easier to write about things than to say them.

J. B. PRIESTLEY

❧

In the novel, the emotion has to be attached to a human being, and the human being has to be attached to a particular time and place, and has to do with other human beings and be involved with them.

PHILIP LARKIN

No novel can be criticized simply on the basis of its subject matter; you have to look to the way in which the subject matter is handled.

ADAM LIVELY

❧

Sentences must stir in the book like leaves in a forest, each distinct from each despite their resemblance.

GUSTAVE FLAUBERT

❧

I look for characters to come alive on the pages; people I can care about, whose tragedies touch me and whose triumphs make me rejoice . . .

SANDRA COHEN

❧

All normal people require both classics and trash.

GEORGE BERNARD SHAW

❧

Personally I found myself asking four questions about every book: Could I read it? If I could read it, did I believe it? If I believed it, did I care about it? And if I cared about it, what was the quality of my caring, and would it last?

PHILIP LARKIN

On Literary Endeavour

It is unwise ever to give a publisher an outline . . . it is like playing the proposed themes of a symphony with one finger.

ANTHONY BURGESS

<hr />

An editor is one who separated the wheat from the chaff, then printed the chaff.

ADLAI STEVENSON

<hr />

I have to drive myself into the nasty bits of writing. It's like climbing a steep hill, forcing your legs all the way. It can be extraordinarily unpleasant. Though the view can be wonderful.

MARGARET DRABBLE

The demands of life are nearly always antithetical to the demands of art. The crying baby does not exactly enhance the daydreaming state needed for writing poems.

ERICA JONG

. . . if a particular thought should prove difficult to insert somewhere, copy it down in the diary without being delayed by the wish to introduce it at one particular point.

DAVID MAMET

We can all learn from Dickens. 'What will happen to Pickwick next week?' 'I don't know, Madam, I haven't written it.'

SOURCE UNKNOWN

Every sentence beginning 'we think you've written a wonderful screenplay' ends with a request for extensive rewrites . . .

ALAN PLATER

On Literary Endeavour

The great thing about not having studied literature is that you don't think obscurity is profound.

VIKRAM SETH

❧

We have read your manuscript with boundless delight. If we were to publish your paper, it would be impossible for us to publish any work of a lower standard. And as it is unthinkable that in the next thousand years we shall see its equal we are to our regret compelled to return your divine composition and beg you a thousand times to overlook our short sight and timidity.

CHINESE REJECTION SLIP

❧

The way to get a sentence properly written is to write something and keep changing it . . . You can be mighty sure of one thing . . . if you don't write anything you won't have anything to change.

KENNETH ROBERTS

❧

The most cursory glance at a literary history in the past 150 years swiftly dispels the illusion that books were ever reviewed simply on their merits . . .

GEORGE GISSING

A proper name is a *capital* matter. One can no more change a character's name than one can change his skin . . .

GUSTAVE FLAUBERT

❧

'Research'. . . isn't something finite and clean cut which a writer does before 'getting down to' the book. It's something wider and vaguer than that, a state of mind, a sort of dreaming . . .

SOURCE UNKNOWN

❧

Through fiction the reader can satisfy his curiosity about such enterprises as fighting or falling in love without having to submit himself to the dangers attendant upon them.

VICTOR NELL

❧

Most popular traditional fiction had concerned itself heavily with plot, but plots don't exist in the normal dull living of ordinary people.

ANTHONY BURGESS

❧

Imaginative activity originates from dissatisfaction.

SIGMUND FREUD

On Literary Endeavour

The books on the shelves are the best clue to a person's biography.

MICHAEL GOVE

❧

The one way of tolerating existence is to lose oneself in literature as in a perpetual orgy.

GUSTAVE FLAUBERT

❧

Are we to say that the claustrophobic dramas of Ibsen and Steinbeck are 'limited' by their bourgeois, domestic settings?

ADAM LIVELY

❧

High literary talent, popular appeal and profitability are rare bedfellows.

JOYCE MARLOW

. . . Sometimes what didn't take place was the most important thing that happened.

MARGUERITE DURAS

To write is a solitary and singular act . . .

MARGARET ATWOOD

Research is the policeman who holds up the plot.

SOURCE UNKNOWN

A novel is primarily an entertainment that should primarily entertain its author . . .

ERNEST HEMINGWAY

Packing is like writing – it needs several drafts.

GERALD SEYMOUR

. . . writing is but a different name for conversation.

LAURENCE STERNE

To me it would not be more absurd if the shoemaker were to wait for inspiration, or the tallow-chandler for the divine moment of melting.

ANTHONY TROLLOPE

All bad poetry is sincere.

OSCAR WILDE

Write as if writing to a friend and use as few words as possible.

MURIEL SPARK

A sentence is well written when it is musically perfect.

GUSTAVE FLAUBERT

Their book is their birthright, their prized possession, their ruler, their fortune and their catastrophe. We cannot separate the Jew from the book.

HEINRICH HEINE

Good drama has no stage directions.

DAVID MAMET

❦

In literature . . . the reader has the possibility of filling things in . . . Film doesn't allow that.

GABRIEL GARCÍA MÁRQUEZ

❦

It's a waste of time to read criticism.

GUSTAVE FLAUBERT

❦

Writing is not literature unless it gives to the reader a pleasure which arises not only from the things said, but from the way in which they are said.

STOPFORD A. BROOKE

❦

. . . The addictive excitement of writing novels . . .

ANTHONY TROLLOPE

❦

I don't read novels. Few last.

LESLEY BLANCH

On Literary Endeavour

Far too often readers face a choice between cardboard characters, lumbering lifelessly from bed to bed, and the pseudo intellectual ramblings of authors who write to please only themselves and a few literary friends.

SOURCE UNKNOWN

You can draw any character as near to life as you want, and no offence will be taken provided you say he was attractive to women.

EVELYN WAUGH

Fall asleep reading a good book and you enter a world of dreams; fall asleep in a film and you miss the end.

STEPHEN AMIDON

. . . a script usually gets worse from the first draft on . . .

DAVID MAMET

We must be on our guard against that feverish state called inspiration . . . Everything should be done coldly, with poise.

GUSTAVE FLAUBERT

❧

. . . if enough money was thrown at a book, bestsellerdom beckoned.

SOURCE UNKNOWN

❧

The sole purpose of the novel is to entertain the reader.

ROSE TREMAIN

❧

Design an artefact which is frequently original, non pollutant, biodegradable, portable, silent, easily reproducible, information-retrievable, cheap, imperishable, translatable, accessible, aesthetically appealing, financially appreciable (the last two not invariable) and the answer is the book . . . far from becoming outmoded, it is remarkably resilient and adaptable.

ANTHONY BLOND

❧

From now on booksellers no longer asked if a book was well written. All that mattered was promotion.

DAVID ELLIOT

. . . due attention to the inside of books, and due contempt for the outside, is the proper relation between a man of sense and his books.

EARL OF CHESTERFIELD

. . . I must aim at lucidity, simplicity, and euphony. I have put these three qualities in the order of importance I assigned to them.

W. SOMERSET MAUGHAM

I had marked down in my notebook three characteristics a work of fiction must possess in order to be successful:

1. It must have a precise and suspenseful plot.
2. The author must feel a passionate urge to write it.
3. He must have the conviction, or at least the illusion, that he is the only one who can handle this particular theme.

ISAAC BASHEVIS SINGER

On Knowledge, Discovery and Travel

I have never found any distress that an hour's reading did not relieve.

MONTESQUIEU

❧

I'd say that travelling meant primarily the discovery of towns and landscapes. People came afterward. People I didn't know.

SIMONE DE BEAUVOIR

❧

Travel makes one modest: one sees what a tiny place one occupies in the world.

GUSTAVE FLAUBERT

Education does not mean that one knows more but one behaves differently.

JOHN RUSKIN

❧

Three permanent reasons for reading: the acquisition of wisdom, the enjoyment of art, and the pleasure of entertainment.

T. S. ELIOT

❧

The man who does not read books is merely not born. He can't see, he can't hear; he can't feel in any full sense, he can only eat his dinner.

ARNOLD BENNETT

❧

We do not receive wisdom; we must discover it for ourselves after a journey that no one can take for us or spare us.

MARCEL PROUST

❧

If educated men, who enjoyed Shakespeare and Schubert, could process human beings through ovens, could the humanities be said to humanize?

GEORGE STEINER

. . . Regard reading as a pleasure, and not as a task to be pursued with clenched teeth.

ARTHUR KOESTLER

❧

So it is in travelling, a man must carry knowledge with him if he would bring home knowledge.

SAMUEL JOHNSON

❧

I learn by heart continually, simply to keep the muscles at attention, like a person who tries to do a marathon.

GEORGE STEINER

❧

There is only one way to read, which is to browse in libraries and bookshops, picking up books that attract you, reading only those, dropping them when they bore you, skipping the parts that drag – and never, never reading anything because you feel you ought, or because it is part of a trend or movement.

DORIS LESSING

❧

It is a false hypothesis that what is taught is what is learned.

SOURCE UNKNOWN

On Knowledge, Discovery and Travel

People who do not travel — at any rate, if they are interested in the arts and learning — are miserable folk indeed.

WOLFGANG AMADEUS MOZART

❧

Read for pleasure . . . never force yourself to read a book — it is a wasted effort . . . If you don't feel that it has a direct bearing on your own personal interests, worries, problems — put it away.

ARTHUR KOESTLER

❧

What would I learn from those wonderful newspapers you so want me to take each morning with my bread and butter and cup of coffee?

GUSTAVE FLAUBERT

Travel is the saddest of the pleasures.

PAUL THEROUX

❧

We cannot be taught wisdom, we have to discover it for ourselves by a journey which no one can undertake for us, our effort which no one can spare us.

ALAIN DE BOTTON

❧

The greatest gift is the passion for reading. It is cheap, it consoles, it distracts, it excites, it gives you knowledge of the world and experience of a wide kind. It is a moral illumination.

ANTHONY BURGESS

On Knowledge, Discovery and Travel

There is nothing we cannot learn from Shakespeare if we will only trust him.

SIMONE DE BEAUVOIR

❧

True education induces a spirit of critical independence and true art is likewise often disturbing, challenging individual preconceptions and social and political conventions.

SIR ROY SHAW

❧

The idea that one can read books without having passed any exams is quite foreign to most young people.

DORIS LESSING

❧

I keep my books round the corner, in the British Museum.

SAMUEL BUTLER

❧

Genius is partly a matter of choice.

COLIN WILSON

❧

It is a wretched pupil who does not surpass his master.

LEONARDO DA VINCI

I think that the true, deepest pleasure of reading comes only from books that do nothing useful for us.

BERNARD LEVIN

❧

The world is a book and those who do not travel read only one page.

ST AUGUSTINE

❧

. . . his [Gustave Flaubert's] preferred form of travel was to lie on a divan and have the scenery carried past him.

SOURCE UNKNOWN

❧

Intellectuals are people who are simply interested in ideas . . .

ISAIAH BERLIN

❧

A man always makes himself greater as he increases his knowledge.

SAMUEL JOHNSON

❧

A clever girl needs the corrective of a humbler soul's wisdom.

GERMAINE GREER

An intellectual person whose interests in and preoccupation with the spiritual side of life are insistent and constant.

ALEXANDER SOLZHENITSYN

Reading books may be dangerous because in them we may find all kinds of images to trouble the souls and change the hearts of men.

ANATOLE FRANCE

Life is but a journey; to travel is to live twice.

SOURCE UNKNOWN

Read. Do not brood. Immerse yourself in long study: only the habit of persistent work can make one continually content.

GUSTAVE FLAUBERT

Humility goes hand in hand with knowledge. Only a person of superficial knowledge will be arrogant.

RABBI JULIAN JACOBS

We cannot teach another person directly. We can only facilitate his learning.

SOURCE UNKNOWN

Civilized nations open libraries.

JOHN MAJOR

Libraries and reading: 'the university that all can enter and none need leave'.

KING GEORGE V

There are two possible sorts of reader. The one who reads purely for pleasure and the other who reads for moral instruction.

LEON YUDKIN

❦

My favourite journey is anywhere I haven't been. Every time I return from a trip, I come back enriched with experiences, new inspirations and a fresh outlook.

DONNA KARAN

❦

What a man cannot learn by literary instinct, and cannot acquire by literary habit, he will never, never be able to obtain from rules and books.

LAFCADIO HEARN

❦

Education has produced a vast population able to read, but unable to distinguish what is worth reading.

G. M. TREVELYAN

❦

Reading maketh a full man; conference a ready man and writing an exact man.

FRANCIS BACON

As hopeless at history as Mrs Disraeli, who did not know whether the Greeks came before or after the Romans.

SOURCE UNKNOWN

I travel in order to travel.

GEORGE SAND

What a bore it is to go out when one would much rather stay home.

MARCEL PROUST

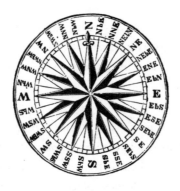

On Creativity and the Arts

An artist needs time to do nothing but sit around and think and let ideas come to him.

GERTRUDE STEIN

The more perfect the artist the more completely separate in him will be the man who suffers and the mind which creates.

T. S. ELIOT

Imagination may produce fears and anxieties, but they also produce music, art and literature.

SOURCE UNKNOWN

. . . they write criticism because they are unable to be artists, just as a man unfit to bear arms becomes a police spy . . . Criticism occupies the lowest place in the literary hierarchy; as regards form, almost always; and as regards 'moral value', incontestably. It comes after rhyming games and acrostics, which at least require a certain inventiveness.

GUSTAVE FLAUBERT

Even musical comedy in the hands of a master might become a thing of beauty.

ARTHUR QUILLER-COUCH

❧

A work of art is not *about* this or that kind of life; it *has* life.

W. H. AUDEN

. . . only a fool would assert that there is no more on Rembrandt's canvas than paint, nothing on Mozart's music paper than notes.

SIMONE DE BEAUVOIR

❧

Art is what you do on Tuesday morning.

JAMES MICHENER

Painters are torn between the exhilarating necessity of painting the picture they believe is possible, and the patent failure of what they do, however successful in the eyes of the world, to meet their own requirements.

FRANCIS BACON

❧

Art is a cheat.

LEO TOLSTOY

❧

Sensation is everything. Art theory essentially useless.

SOURCE UNKNOWN

❧

The muse ushers the artist into the empty room and points silently at the tightrope.

JEAN COCTEAU

❧

People look to the arts to supplement their lives.

FRANCIS WHEEN

❧

Great art is seldom made in the blinking of an eye.

SOURCE UNKNOWN

. . . men have been outraged on discovering, as they so often have, the discrepancy between the artist's life and his work.

W. SOMERSET MAUGHAM

❧

Even a movie shown on television is a second-hand, second-rate experience, on a par with watching edited highlights of the Sistine Chapel ceiling.

ALAN PLATER

❧

Domestic life and art do not mix easily.

SOURCE UNKNOWN

❧

Great artists are seldom great talkers . . .

ANTHONY STORR

❧

All experience is useful to an artist.

WALTER DE LA MARE

❧

Harmony is an intellectual exercise by those who do not understand melody.

SOURCE UNKNOWN

On Creativity and the Arts

Sooner or later, every artist encounters rejection . . .

ERICA JONG

❧

Authentic art has no use for proclamations, it accomplishes its work in silence.

MARCEL PROUST

Would a musician feel flattered by the loud applause of his audience if it were known to him that with the exception of one or two it consisted largely of deaf people?

ARTHUR SCHOPENHAUER

❧

The critic's task is to set a novel in the context of social history, to analyse and not to judge.

SOURCE UNKNOWN

Every artist has but one *oeuvre*.

MARCEL PROUST

Politics in a work of art is like a pistol shot at a concert.

STENDHAL

Contrary to the bohemian stereotype, the true artist is highly organized and must constantly select and order her material, choosing only that which can be shaped to an ultimate purpose.

JEANETTE WINTERSON

I advise you when composing to consider not only the musical but also the unmusical public. You must remember that to every ten real connoisseurs there are a hundred ignoramuses.

LEOPOLD MOZART

Artistic talent cannot be created, only developed.

CAMILLE PAGLIA

❧

The life of an artist is a long road to Calvary.

PAUL GAUGUIN

❧

Extraordinary how potent cheap music is.

NOËL COWARD

❧

Pay no attention to what the critics say: no statue has ever been put up to a critic.

JEAN SIBELIUS

❧

The more we study art, the less we care for nature.

OSCAR WILDE

❧

To be altogether true to his spiritual life an artist must remain alone and not be prodigal of himself, even to disciples. The artist is not another citizen, a social creature with social duties; he is a solitary explorer, a pure egotist.

MARCEL PROUST

Many artists, both first-rate and second-rate, have now been analysed and the results have been unequivocal. When the artistic impulse is genuine the greater freedom achieved through analysis has heightened the artistic capacity, but when to wish to become an artist is impelled by purely neurotic and irrelevant motives, the analysis clarifies the situation.

ERNEST JONES

I think art has no purpose. The purpose of art is to be art.

ISAIAH BERLIN

I think art has no purpose. The purpose of art is to be art.

We are all actors who cannot become something before we have first pretended to be it.

W. H. AUDEN

On Creativity and the Arts

Creative people are often astonished by what they have produced, and treat it sometimes as if someone else had produced it.

ANTHONY STORR

❧

There is no such uniform entity as 'The critics'. There are only individuals reporting their independent responses to an artistic experience.

SOURCE UNKNOWN

❧

He knew that to be torn between tears and laughter is the best experience the theatre can offer.

GYÖRGY LIGETI

❧

Artists have to be religious, if by religious one means believing that life has some significance and some meaning which is what I think it has. An artist couldn't work without believing that.

HENRY MOORE

❧

The roots of art and play lie very close together.

ANGUS WILSON

'Back-scratching' the canaille call it. To Americans it is 'log-rolling'. With a sensuality for which he is too seldom given credit, Leavis referred to it as 'flank-rubbing'. Quality newspapers call it 'Books of the Year'.

HOWARD JACOBSON

⭕⚜⭕

No work of art is ever finished – only abandoned.

PAUL VALÉRY

⭕⚜⭕

The main purpose of art is to give pleasure.

MURIEL SPARK

⭕⚜⭕

In Art as in Love, give yourself away.

SOURCE UNKNOWN

⭕⚜⭕

She [Vela] didn't give a shit about Gothic architecture or stained glass.

SAUL BELLOW

⭕⚜⭕

Concentrate on the craft and the art will take care of itself.

DAVID MAMET

Those who have become eminent in philosophy, politics, poetry, and the arts have all had tendencies toward melancholia.

ARISTOTLE

Reviewing is a whole-time job with a half-time salary, a job in which the best in him is generally expended on to the mediocre in others.

W. SOMERSET MAUGHAM

You do not become cultured by being led in a crowd round an art gallery; you recede in fact from culture therefore your own perceptions are atrophied by standards imposed on them.

A. J. AYER

When a producer says 'trust me', that's the time to get it in writing.

SOURCE UNKNOWN

L'oeuvre d'art, c'est une idée qu'on exagère.

ANDRÉ GIDE

༺❦༻

A critic is a man who knows the way but can't drive a car.

KENNETH TYNAN

༺❦༻

Whatever moments of excellence it achieves, television is a natural enemy of the other arts and has almost overwhelmed them. It has taught us to be impatient.

MICHAEL HOLROYD

༺❦༻

Music gives us the quickest insight into reality.

SOURCE UNKNOWN

༺❦༻

Covent Garden audiences look as if Harrods Food Hall has yielded up its dead.

JONATHAN MILLER

༺❦༻

One of our contemporaries is cured of his torment, simply by contemplating a landscape.

ALBERT CAMUS

On Creativity and the Arts

There is never anything on television, it is all a load of hogwash these days.

SIR JOHN MORTIMER

❧

You keep talking about art and all I'm interested in is the money.

GEORGE BERNARD SHAW

❧

'The MacGuffin'. This was, of course, Hitchcock's term for 'that which the hero wants' and his devotion to the concept explains much of his success as a film director.

DAVID MAMET

. . . the first performance of Mozart's *Marriage of Figaro* was booed in Vienna . . . when the Impressionists first showed their work they were laughed at.

MORDECHAI RICHLER

. . . Mozart goes down to a level from which no traveller returns, or wishes to; for one who has really understood Mozart, life can never be the same again.

BERNARD LEVIN

❧

Picasso, when asked why he was always to be found on the balcony, painting the same view, replied: 'Because every moment the light is different, the colours are different, the atmosphere is different.'

❧

Television is a fantasy which destroys everything.

MALCOLM MUGGERIDGE

❧

To catalogue the individual distinction of the C minor Symphony is akin to counting the stones in the Taj Mahal or measuring the length of the nose of the Mona Lisa. It is the composite that counts.

SOURCE UNKNOWN

❧

The main media of the country are sewers, for me they're where much of the filth in our culture gets poured out.

JOHN FOWLES

A man now has his best relationship with some man on the TV screen, not with his wife or son. You are watching trees on the screen and not in nature. Satellite TV is the most sacrificial of all; you see everything and feel nothing . . .

IVAN KLIMA

Without art a man may find his life on earth unliveable.

FYODOR DOSTOYEVSKY

. . . television has made us extraordinarily well informed on subjects we know nothing about.

MICHAEL HOLROYD

Michelangelo, Goethe, Rembrandt, Victor Hugo, Titian, Immanuel Kant, Rabelais, Benjamin Franklin all did their best work long after middle age.

SOURCE UNKNOWN

We are told that there are great photographers . . . But I cannot for the life of me see how mere recording can be creation . . .

ANTHONY BURGESS

❦

In art, as in everything else, truth comes from within.

BERNARD LEVIN

Off-stage characters have a way of enriching a cast at no extra cost to the management . . .

DAVID CAMPTON

❦

A man's style in any art should be like his dress – it should attract as little attention as possible.

SAMUEL BUTLER

❦

Criticism is the literature of our time.

SOURCE UNKNOWN

... what I resent is that whenever you turn on the television you find people screaming at each other in their kitchens. People don't want to watch that. They want something different from their everyday lives. They want to see an attractive drawing room.

DAME BARBARA CARTLAND

❧

The 'television personality' who possesses no skill other than a quick wit and a certain ease of manner in public, is a modern phenomenon which has never existed before.

ANTHONY STORR

❧

In the arts their audience would be the inevitably small minority of truly cultivated people as opposed to the mob, who wished only to be entertained or to be assured they were 'cultured'. By now ... the mob was better known as the middle class.

TOM WOLFE

❧

You can make a film about falling *in* love, you can make a film about falling *out* of love, but you can't make a film about being *in* love – too boring.

SYDNEY POLLACK

[123]

Any discussion of art is almost always rubbish and is just intended to keep people in jobs in universities. If you've written something that comes out well you don't think 'Ah art' you just think of it as a job well done.

AUBERON WAUGH

❧

The main concerns of Art are ideas and concepts – not methods and techniques.

SOURCE UNKNOWN

❧

One must die to life to be more of an artist.

RILKE

❧

TV plunges people into noisy isolation.

FRANÇOISE SAGAN

❧

I don't like revealing sex on the stage, not because I'm a prude but because sex needs to be described from the inside as a poet or novelist can do, and, when it is shown from the outside, with solid bodies on the stage, we are turned into voyeurs.

J. B. PRIESTLEY

The crucial moments in a film should be wordless if possible.

SATYAJIT RAY

❦

Michelangelo didn't jump up full grown and do the Sistine Chapel – he worked as an apprentice with another painter for seven years. Beethoven learned to write his own music by studying with Haydn and other composers . . . Guy de Maupassant learned from Flaubert . . .

RAYMOND CARVER

Creativity has been defined . . . 'as the ability to bring something new into existence'.

ANTHONY STORR

❦

Film and TV purvey life to those who do not live it.

SOURCE UNKNOWN

In my view, the only works of art that should be considered beautiful are those that have contributed, or contribute, to the making of a better world.

JEAN GIMPEL

❦

. . . the critic secretly wants to kill the writer. . . . we all hate golden eggs. Bloody golden eggs again, you can hear the critics mutter as a good novelist produces yet another good novel; haven't we had enough omelettes this year?

GUSTAVE FLAUBERT

❦

. . . audiences still come to the London theatre to discover who they are.

SOURCE UNKNOWN

❦

Creativity . . . producing ostensibly out of nothing, something of beauty, order or significance.

SIR PETER MEDAWAR

❦

Tolstoy maintained that if a piece of art could not be understood by the most lumpen peasant then it wasn't art.

SOURCE UNKNOWN

The Beatles were rejected by Decca and the Monopoly game was originally written off by Parker Brothers.

SOURCE UNKNOWN

I felt passionately about not wanting my children watching TV because it was vulgar, stupid and debasing.

AUBERON WAUGH

You can make a perfectly decent living writing for films that never get made.

FREDERICK RAPHAEL

The review should set out to present what the author has to say, to decide whether he has done what he set out to do, and where he has failed, and finally to add any personal points that seem germane to the discussion of the book.

SOURCE UNKNOWN

On the Human Condition

The world of Imagination is the world of eternity.

WILLIAM BLAKE

❧

Simple records of fact bear no fruit. They do not warm the heart and throw no light on the human condition.

SOURCE UNKNOWN

❧

. . . not that I rank marriage or success in a profession as success. It's an attitude of mind — the way one looks at life.

VIRGINIA WOOLF

On the Human Condition

It was he [Voltaire] who taught three generations that superstition was ridiculous, sentiment absurd, fanaticism unintelligent and oppression infamous.

HAROLD NICOLSON

❧

It is no sin to be neurotic.

SIGMUND FREUD

❧

In solitude the lonely man is eaten up by himself, among crowds by the many. Choose which you prefer.

FRIEDRICH NIETZSCHE

❧

. . . sexual relations without an emotional bond degrade . . .

ARTHUR SCHNITZLER

❧

Take away my nervous exaltation, my fantasy of mind, the emotion of the moment, and I have little left.

GUSTAVE FLAUBERT

❧

Making money does not seem to me a very elevating ambition.

SIMONE DE BEAUVOIR

A washing machine never made any woman happy.

FRANÇOISE SAGAN

Eccentricity is seldom more than the acceptable face of egotism . . .

FRANCIS KING

The soul of man is a far country, which cannot be approached or explored.

D. M. THOMAS

Getting upset is a personal choice.

PETER NIXON

On the Human Condition

If I am not for myself, who is for me? But if I am only for myself, what am I? And if not now, when?

RABBI HILLEL

❦

Do you feel happiness is unlikely in this world? Well, I think if you're in good health, and have enough money, and nothing is bothering you in the foreseeable future that's as much as you can hope for.

PHILIP LARKIN

❦

You'll understand later that one keeps on forgetting old age up to the very brink of the grave.

SOURCE UNKNOWN

❦

So many youngsters confuse lack of discipline with independence.

ELIE WIESEL

❦

. . . she found it hard to cope with visitors without Harold [Nicolson] there to mediate and talk; she told him she felt decreased by talking while others are increased.

VITA SACKVILLE-WEST

I find social intercourse fatiguing. Most persons . . . are both exhilarated and rested by conversation; to me it has always been an effort . . . it is a strain. It is a relief to me when I can get away and read a book.

VIRGINIA WOOLF

It is only shallow people who do not judge by appearances. The mystery of the world is the visible, not the invisible.

OSCAR WILDE

What is wrong with being obsessed with trivia?

BARBARA PYM

What man cannot get by flying he can get by limping.

SIGMUND FREUD

On the Human Condition

But incessant stimulation from without is a source of bondage; and so is the preoccupation with possessions.

ALDOUS HUXLEY

❧

It is always the man who is revealed in his work.

ELIE WIESEL

❧

Most young people think they are being natural when really they are just ill-mannered and crude.

LA ROCHEFOUCAULD

❧

Hierarchy is what destroys people's personal value. Being above or below is absurd.

SIMONE DE BEAUVOIR

❧

Use every man after his desert and who shall 'scape whipping.

WILLIAM SHAKESPEARE

❧

People always call me a feminist when I express opinions which differentiate me from a doormat.

REBECCA WEST

To be without some of the things you want is an essential part of happiness.

BERTRAND RUSSELL

Women who say they are indifferent to clothes, like men who say they do not mind what they eat, should be distrusted: there is something wrong.

J. B. PRIESTLEY

Be regular and orderly in your life like a bourgeois, so that you may be violent and original in your work.

GUSTAVE FLAUBERT

The Human psyche has no colour, no slant of the eye . . .

SOURCE UNKNOWN

Sooner or later in life everyone discovers that perfect happiness is unrealizable, but there are few who pause to consider the antithesis: that perfect unhappiness is equally unattainable.

PRIMO LEVI

❦

Women are humorous and satirical rather than imaginative.

VIRGINIA WOOLF

❦

I enjoy solitude the way some people I know enjoy parties. It gives me an enormous sense of being alive.

PHILIP ROTH

❦

You can't control what other people do, only the way you *react* to what they do. If other people annoy you, it is not they who are being annoying, it is you who are being annoyed.

SOURCE UNKNOWN

❦

Not all creative people are notably disturbed; not all solitary people are unhappy.

ANTHONY STORR

Old age is a shipwreck.

CHARLES DE GAULLE

ॐ

. . . when one is messy in small things one is messy in big ones . . .

SIMONE DE BEAUVOIR

ॐ

No man will ever unfold the capacities of his own intellect, who does not at least checker his life with solitude.

THOMAS DE QUINCEY

ॐ

Morning's a good time!

COLETTE

ॐ

The modern mind is over-congested, tired to death of keeping up.

SAUL BELLOW

ॐ

Our bones spread. The knit of our flesh loosens, no matter how we diet.

JOHN UPDIKE

Just as half the trick of being a good cook is knowing how to shop properly – which bits of meat and which vegetables to choose from all the others – so a large part of being a good novelist is knowing which bits of experience to discard.

A. N. WILSON

We must reserve a little back-shop, all our own, entirely free, wherein to establish our true liberty and principal retreat and solitude.

MONTAIGNE

Depression was not tears. It was deadness. Immobility. A black hole.

DORIS LESSING

Most people are mediocre, and want to see their mediocrity mirrored in print.

ANTHONY BURGESS

❦

Every time a friend is successful a little part of me dies.

GORE VIDAL

❦

My dear, I don't care what they do, so long as they don't do it in the street and frighten the horses.

MRS PATRICK CAMPBELL

The world is a comedy to those who think, a tragedy to those who feel.

HORACE WALPOLE

❦

Many live wires would be dead were it not for their connections.

JOCK MURRAY

Friendship flags unless it is kept warm.

SIR SYDNEY COCKERELL

※

You will never be happy if you continue to search for what happiness consists of. You will never live if you are looking for the meaning of life.

ALBERT CAMUS

※

. . . it was important to note how people looked . . . If you don't take into account their haircuts, the hang of their pants, their taste in skirts and blouses, their style of driving a car or eating a dinner, your knowledge is incomplete.

SAUL BELLOW

※

Domestic misfortunes are the only serious misfortunes.

WILKIE COLLINS

※

I live in a constant state of over-excitement; so much do my work and conception thrill me. It is almost too much for me and I am always feeling rather ill. One seems to work at the expense of one's body and there is no other way of doing it.

MARK GERTLER

We live as we dream – alone.

JOSEPH CONRAD

❧

Socially I am a cripple.

VLADIMIR NABOKOV

❧

Sex is totally ludicrous to everybody except the participants.

ALAN PLATER

❧

A man, Sir, should keep his friendship in constant repair.

SAMUEL JOHNSON

❧

. . . Fine clothes are out of place when a woman is no longer young.

STENDHAL

❧

When he was hungry, he thought of soup and not of immortality. After a long night's march, he yearned for rest and not for mercy. Was this all there was to man?

ELIE WIESEL

The worst thing about getting old is feeling young.

OSCAR WILDE

❧

Suddenly we realize how, all our lives, we have been trained to appease and flatter men, how not to confront them.

ERICA JONG

❧

Alas, after a certain age every man is responsible for his face.

ALBERT CAMUS

❧

. . . a person going through puberty must first reject everything he once loved in order to establish new values for himself.

ALICE MILLER

Discussion presupposes a calm, level-headed exchange of views.

CAROLINE BAILEY

❧

In earlier days I never used to worry about old people; I looked upon them as the dead whose legs still kept moving. Now I see them – men and women: only a little older than myself . . .

SIMONE DE BEAUVOIR

. . . simple, sober truth has no chance whatever of being listened to, and it's only by volume of shouting that the ear of the public is held . . .

GEORGE GISSING

❧

Human beings are interested in other human beings.

DAVID CAMPTON

On the Human Condition

I know of no man of genius who had not to pay, in some affliction or defect either spiritual or physical, for what the gods had given him.

MAX BEERBOHM

❧

We are like anyone else only more so.

JEAN-PAUL SARTRE

❧

If I do not rouse my soul to higher things who will rouse it?

MAIMONIDES

❧

I'm growing old. It isn't nice, but it's interesting.

AUGUST STRINDBERG

❧

You see I do not aim to be great at all in anything, but perhaps I may be reasonably happy in my work.

WILLIAM MORRIS

❧

What you failed to do when you were young you can't make up for later.

AHARON APPELFELD

Nothing can be created without loneliness. I have created a loneliness for myself which nobody can comprehend. It is very difficult to be alone! There are clocks and watches.

PABLO PICASSO

❧

In the morning, solitude.

PYTHAGORAS

❧

Il faut cultiver notre jardin.

VOLTAIRE

❧

I am a poor guest and dislike staying in other people's houses.

GORE VIDAL

❧

. . . Political Commitment . . . can kill creative impulse.

GEORGE ORWELL

To act boastfully about something we should be ashamed of. That's a trick that never seems to fail.

JOSEPH HELLER

❧

What have I in common with the Jews? I have hardly anything in common with myself and should stand very quietly in a corner, content that I can breathe.

FRANZ KAFKA

❧

We can never be sure that the opinion we are endeavouring to stifle is a false opinion; and if we were sure, stifling it would be an evil still . . . All silencing of discussion is an assumption of infallibility.

JOHN STUART MILL

❧

I've never been anywhere where I felt comfortable. I've always been hanging about looking for somewhere or for something to do.

MARGUERITE DURAS

❧

Work is much more fun than fun.

NOËL COWARD

The crowd has taken possession of places, which were created by civilization for the minority, for the best people.

José Ortega y Gasset

❧

Life is a well of delight; but where the rabble also drink, there all fountains are poisoned.

Friedrich Nietzsche

❧

I have never liked parties of any kind . . . and the grander they are the less I have liked them.

Gore Vidal

. . . we must learn the difference between rejecting an opinion expressed by an individual, and rejecting the individual himself.

Rabbi Shmuel Boteach

We act as though comfort and luxury were the chief requirements of life, when all we need to make us really happy is something to be enthusiastic about.

CHARLES KINGSLEY

❧

To be ignorant of what occurred before you were born is to remain always a child.

CICERO

❧

When I dance, I dance; when I sleep, I sleep . . .

MONTAIGNE

❧

Humankind cannot bear too much reality.

T. S. ELIOT

❧

Power is the ultimate aphrodisiac.

HENRY KISSINGER

❧

Don't stop doing things when you're growing old, because you'll only grow old when you stop doing things.

DAME THORA HIRD

Of the greatest importance in our lives . . . are festive occasions, when we join with other people in doing purposeless things.

ROGER SCRUTON

❧

Most men and more women – young women afraid for themselves – punish older women with derision.

DORIS LESSING

❧

Everybody thinks of changing humanity. Nobody thinks of changing himself.

LEO TOLSTOY

❧

'A man,' said he, 'must have a very good opinion of himself when he asks people to leave their own fireside . . . for the sake of coming to see him . . . The folly is not allowing people to be comfortable at home, and the folly of people's not staying comfortably at home when they can . . .'

JANE AUSTEN

❧

A definition of moral progress is the realization that other human beings are as fully human as oneself.

PHILIP TOYNBEE

'Red or white?' The three most boring words in the English language.

SIR KINGSLEY AMIS

❧

At my age . . . life I may say melts in the hand . . . I sit down, just arrange my thoughts, peep out of the window, turn over a page and it's bedtime.

VIRGINIA WOOLF

❧

If you perceive people straightforwardly as themselves, there is no need to idealize them. That only happens when the feeling is negative.

STEPHEN LANG

❧

A cynic always hides his true feelings.

SOURCE UNKNOWN

The truth is, I like it when people actually come; but I love it when they go.

VIRGINIA WOOLF

People might occasionally enjoy solitude but never loneliness; they need to feel connected and valued.

MONTAIGNE

He never wasted time: he . . . 'accomplished the business of the day within the day'.

DUKE OF WELLINGTON

. . . you can't sing the blues if you haven't had the blues.

DAVID MAMET

On the Human Condition

We all walk on very thin ice. We all pretend we don't, but we know how easy it is for our present happiness to be shattered.

WILLIAM BOYD

❧

Koestler worried that he was too old to make new friends, fearing that there was not enough time to amass the hinterland of shared experiences that bound people together.

DAVID CESARANI

❧

Counselling has become the resource of the unqualified female – it has replaced the sewing machine.

DORIS LESSING

❧

One day everything will be well, that is our hope; today everything is fine, that is our illusion.

VOLTAIRE

❧

'How old would you say I was?'
'I've no idea.'
'Eighty-one.' He waited for some rebuttal.

ANITA BROOKNER

We must be as courteous to a man, as we are to a picture,
which we are willing to give the advantage of a good light.

RALPH WALDO EMERSON

All cruel people describe themselves as paragons of frankness.

TENNESSEE WILLIAMS

Sex at the right time, with the right person under the right
circumstances is just about the most tremendous experience
human beings can know.

SOURCE UNKNOWN

Friendship is the supreme human relationship.

ARISTOTLE

Our frankness invites a reciprocal frankness, and draws forth discoveries, like wine and love.

MONTAIGNE

❧

Racism will end when individuals see others only in individual terms. 'There are no "white" or "colored" signs on the graveyards of battle.'

JOHN F. KENNEDY

❧

. . . if you hate a person, you hate something in him that is part of yourself.

HERMANN HESSE

❧

Every reproach can hurt only to the extent that it hits the mark. Whoever actually knows that he does not deserve a reproach can and will confidently treat it with contempt.

ARTHUR SCHOPENHAUER

❧

The way I feel about books on sex is the way I feel about other people's holiday snaps; who wants to look at other people doing what you'd rather be doing yourself.

SOURCE UNKNOWN

He was at an age when most men retired, and no doubt they were all faced with the same daunting prospect. So much time! How on earth was it to be filled?

ANITA BROOKNER

❧

Freud's dictum that it is easier to promote goodwill between two groups if there is a third they can both hate.

AMOS ELON

❧

I am always surprised to see some people demanding the time of others and meeting a most obliging response . . . neither regards the time itself — as if nothing there is being asked for and nothing given. They are trifling with life's most precious commodity.

SENECA

I have to be alone for some time every day then I'm a nicer person.

DAVID HARE

oɤo

My solution to disappointments is to keep so many balls in the air – it doesn't matter if some fall . . .

SIR JOHN MORTIMER

oɤo

When we cease laying blame we either take responsibility for our own contributions, or become free to recognize that blame is irrelevant: for such things happen as part of the whirligig of life and laying blame is a waste of energy which could be better directed at repairing damages or starting afresh.

MONTAIGNE

oɤo

It's easy to get the mob to agree with you; all you have to do is agree with the mob.

WILLIAM HAZLITT

oɤo

Nous sommes venus trop tard dans un monde trop vieux.

LA BRUYÈRE

Growing old is no more than a bad habit which a busy man has no time to form.

ANDRÉ MAUROIS

ॐ

We are all guilty of hammering on the knuckles of those who try to climb into our boat.

BETTY MILLER

ॐ

Almost always extra-marital sex is a symptom, a reflection of some kind of basic emptiness in the life of the person . . .

SOURCE UNKNOWN

ॐ

Flexibility of attitudes and beliefs is hugely important, and helps keep you young and engaged with the world.

MICHAEL CRICHTON

ॐ

What is the harm in returning to the point whence you came?

SENECA

ॐ

I can live for two months on a good compliment.

MARK TWAIN

Our sexual education of children was like sending them on a polar expedition equipped with summer clothing and images of the Italian lakes.

SIGMUND FREUD

❧

There may be not better way to clear the diary of engagements than to wonder who among our acquaintances would make the trip to the hospital bed.

AMOS OZ

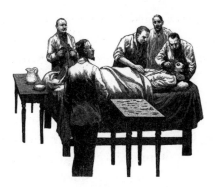

It has wisely been said that the search for happiness is one of the main sources of unhappiness in the world.

MONTAIGNE

❧

Fate waits around every corner with a sock full of wet sand.

P. G. WODEHOUSE

A man should not talk about himself unless it carries some meaning for others. To speak about yourself just because something has happened to you is foolishness or worse still pure selfishness.

AHARON APPELFELD

❧

Let no one rob me of a single day who is not going to make me an adequate return for such a loss.

SENECA

❧

Our virtues are but mostly vices in disguise.

LA ROCHEFOUCAULD

❧

However wisely a foolishly modern parent treats sex education, the sort of innocence my generation knew has by now become an emotional impossibility.

DERVLA MURPHY

❧

. . . so gradually in Western democracies the panic over losing a washing machine has acquired the same kind of fear that hunger held in harsher times.

ARIANNA STASSINOPOLOUS

One must try to temper, to cut, to polish one's soul so as to become a human being.

ALEXANDER SOLZHENITSYN

❧

Morality and happiness go hand in hand. Immoral behaviour makes people miserable . . . not right away in some cases perhaps, but by and large sooner or later.

SOURCE UNKNOWN

Sometimes I have been driven by my desire to seek the company of other human beings, but what humiliation when someone, standing beside me, heard a flute from afar off while I heard nothing, or when someone heard a shepherd singing and again I heard nothing! Such experiences have brought me close to despair . . .

LUDWIG VAN BEETHOVEN

Sex is the means whereby one person can reach another at the deepest level and at the same time discover new things about himself.

SOURCE UNKNOWN

Silence is the real crime against humanity.

NADEZHDA MANDELSTAM

Man is so made by nature as to require him to restrict his movements as far as his hands and feet will take him.

MAHATMA GANDHI

There is no total honesty without hurting.

SOURCE UNKNOWN

Loneliness is the world's most serious problem. It affects people in country or town; married or single. Often it is linked to shyness or needs professional care.

MOTHER TERESA OF CALCUTTA

❧

For human beings, sexuality can be and often is a way of bonding, of giving and receiving pleasure, bridging different-ness, discovering sameness, and communicating emotion.

GLORIA STEINEM

❧

As you well know I am a man given to great *élans* and deep discouragement.

GUSTAVE FLAUBERT

❧

Doomed to mediocrity we are humbled by transcendent minds.

MONTESQUIEU

❧

It has become publicly acceptable for men to label a woman first as a feminist and then as a lesbian. By doing so they effectively isolate her from the human race.

ERIN PIZZEY

To refuse to do any more work today than you are paid for is one of the greatest obstacles to advancement and success.

PETER BULOS

❧

Every face has a fixed look, which is not only based on the formation of the features themselves, but is also moulded by the qualities of the inner spirit.

ALAN SILLITOE

❧

To judge every man in the scale of merit, to give people the benefit of the doubt, is a praiseworthy quality.

RABBI ISAIAH HOROWITZ

❧

To be well dressed, everyone must dress in a way best suited to himself.

GUSTAVE FLAUBERT

❧

. . . Even in an insane world it is still possible to live decently, even nobly. It is not finally a matter of skill, of knowledge, of intellect; of good luck or bad, but choosing and learning to feel.

JOHN FOWLES

On the Human Condition

Age does not count, what counts is passion and liking what one does.

CLAUDIO ABBADO

❧

Just as the faces of humans are different, so are their thoughts and opinions.

MAIMONIDES

❧

No one is born hating another person because of the colour of his skin . . . People must learn to hate, and if they can learn to hate, they can be taught to love, for love comes more naturally to a human heart than its opposite.

NELSON MANDELA

Learning, thinking, innovation and maintaining contract with one's own inner world are all facilitated by solitude.

ANTHONY STORR

❧

Have great objectives in view, but keep them secret.

PETER BULOS

❧

All that is necessary for the triumph of evil is that good men do nothing.

EDMUND BURKE

❧

Si jeunesse savait; si vieillesse pouvait.

HENRI ESTIENNE

. . . most of society's rules dictate that man must be central or he will sulk.

ERICA JONG

❦

Men are like fires. If you don't feed them they go out.

MAE WEST

❦

Race has no biological reality: . . . race is a social, cultural and political concept based on superficial appearances and historical conditions . . . there is simply no such thing as 'white', 'black' or 'yellow' people; there are people with many shades and types of skin, making no difference to any other aspect of their humanity save what the malice of others can construct.

MONTAIGNE

❦

I stand up for every human being. It's such a welcoming gesture.

SOURCE UNKNOWN

❦

The most dangerous thing is to think logically.

ROMAN VISHNIAC

There is something wrong with a man who does not enjoy his work more and more as he gets older.

PETER BULOS

⚜

Those engaged in its practice [murder] did not belong to a gutter society of misfits . . . Many held degrees in philosophy, sociology, biology, general medicine, psychiatry and the fine arts.

ELIE WIESEL

⚜

Although money is not an emotion, it can produce intensely emotional feelings, which is perhaps why it is considered safer not to talk about it.

CAROLINE BAILEY

⚜

Life as a couple implies decisions 'When shall we eat? What would you like to have? Plans come into being. When one is alone, things happen without premeditation: it is restful.

SIMONE DE BEAUVOIR

⚜

With great talent come great responsibilities.

PHILIP ROTH

Friendships aren't often discussed and brooded over, as love is. Untended, they decay like teeth and fall away – to be replaced by bright false ones, whole dentures of them if necessary.

VICTORIA GLENDINNING

❧

Tout passe, tout lasse, tout casse.

SOURCE UNKNOWN

The sexual act can have a luminous quality which goes beyond intercourse itself.

CAROLINE BAILEY

❧

Excellence is never granted to man, but as a reward of labour.

SIR JOSHUA REYNOLDS

I have never understood why people find it so difficult to speak the truth to their acquaintances and friends . . . People fear to offend or hurt others, not because they are kind, but because they do not care for the truth.

SUSAN SONTAG

To a victim of the 'concentrationary' system, it no longer mattered that he had been an intellectual labourer, angry student or devoted husband. A few beatings, a few screams turned him into a blank, his loss of identity complete.

ELIE WIESEL

There are two good reasons to buy anything, because it's very cheap or because it's very expensive.

COCO CHANEL

The money which a man possesses is the instrument of freedom.

JEAN-JACQUES ROUSSEAU

The failure to create one's own space can have serious consequences, particularly for women. 'Depression as a bid for space and sanctuary has, as yet, gone unrecognized by psychiatrists . . .'

CHRIS BELSHAW/MIKE STRUTT

❧

The ecstasies of sexual sensation are no more to be described than the ecstasies of music they resemble.

V. S. PRITCHETT

❧

Carpe diem cannot be understood by anyone under thirty-five.

SOURCE UNKNOWN

❧

Like many women she was torn between her artistic and her human responsibilities. To be human is more important because it is more needed.

MARINA TSVETAYEVA

❧

I don't like the idea of sitting around at dinner parties parading a few half-baked opinions.

STEVEN BERKOFF

The moral person protests not only when he is personally wronged but also when he witnesses or thinks about the sufferings of others.

ISAAC BASHEVIS SINGER

❧

If all mankind minus one were of one opinion, and only one person were of the contrary opinion, mankind would be no more justified in silencing that one person than he, if had the power, would be justified in silencing mankind.

JOHN STUART MILL

❧

. . . [the] worst day is one frittered away in preconceived responses to the demands of others on my time and energy and psychic space . . . I must have time to stand and stare.

GERMAINE GREER

❧

When I see someone coming towards me with the obvious intention of doing me good, I run a mile.

HENRY DAVID THOREAU

❧

Good sex is like money: if you've got it you don't talk about it.

SOURCE UNKNOWN

Things are not necessarily lovely *behind the façade*, and so it is with human beings too.

SIGMUND FREUD

❧

There is always some discrepancy between an individual's public face and what he is in private.

ANTHONY STORR

❧

The armed struggle was imposed upon us by the violence of the apartheid regime.

NELSON MANDELA

❧

There are two kinds of people in this world; those who do things and those who dream of doing things.

SOURCE UNKNOWN

I try not to go shopping, but when I have to do it I do it on the commando-raid principle – get in, get it and get out.

JEREMY CLARKE

❧

Depression while it lasts is permanent.

BRIAN ALDISS

Amateurs look for inspiration; the rest of us just get up and go to work.

PHILIP ROTH

❧

Men are sometimes free to do what they wish, but they are never free in their wishes.

THOMAS HOBBES

❧

Plus je vais, plus je trouve.

GUSTAVE FLAUBERT

[172]

'I believe that the mob, the mass, the herd will always be despicable' . . . one could not elevate the masses even if one tried.

GUSTAVE FLAUBERT

❧

They [the middle classes] . . . prefer comfort to pleasure, convenience to liberty, and a pleasant temperature to that deathly inner consuming fire.

HERMANN HESSE

❧

A man should learn to detect and watch that gleam of light which flashes across the mind from within, more than the lustre of the firmament of bards and sages.

RALPH WALDO EMERSON

❧

The mind is a strange and funny thing. In the summer it longs for winter, and then in the winter it longs for summer.

SOURCE UNKNOWN

❧

Man was a pauper when it came to reason, but a millionaire when it came to emotions.

ISAAC BASHEVIS SINGER

It's just that I never have much to say so I keep quiet.

ALBERT CAMUS

❧

The only way to forget is to remember.

SIGMUND FREUD

❧

. . . I imagine the mainspring of all our actions is, after all, self-interest.

LEO TOLSTOY

❧

Le monde appartient à ceux qui se lévent tôt.

SOURCE UNKNOWN

When from our better selves we have too long
Been parted by the hurrying world, and droop,
Sick of its business, of its pleasures tired,
How gracious, how benign is Solitude.

WILLIAM WORDSWORTH

Nature without people is meaningless.

SOURCE UNKNOWN

❧

Only great men change their minds.

ADLAI STEVENSON

❧

The man who makes no mistakes does not usually make anything.

WILLIAM CONNOR MAGEE

❧

Some people play brilliantly with poor cards, and others do the opposite; they squander and lose everything with brilliant cards.

AMOS OZ

❧

Belittling others is no pastime for those convinced of their own standing.

ALAIN DE BOTTON

❧

My tastes are very simple. I only like the best.

OSCAR WILDE

On Love, Marriage and Family

The family is the symbol of the last area where one has any hope of control over one's destiny, of meeting one's most basic human needs . . . For the family, psychologists tell us, is the nutriment of our humanness, of all our individuality.

BETTY FRIEDAN

Aristotle's famous view that if children did not love their parents and family members they would love no one but themselves, is one of the most important statements ever made about the relation between family and society.

BRIGITTE BERGER

There is a place for silence as well as conversation in any relationship.

CAROLINE BAILEY

❧

Peace with six children was next to impossible. One would fall ill, another would threaten to fall ill, a third would be without something necessary, a fourth would show symptoms of a bad disposition, and so on, and so on.

LEO TOLSTOY

❧

If you're not prepared to stick it [marriage] out . . . in the mist and rain you'll never see the view from the top of the mountain.

SOURCE UNKNOWN

❧

'Where would I be without my wife?' The humble remark of all great men of this century, from Dumézil to de Gaulle.

MARGUERITE DURAS

❧

Work and love are the only ways in which human nature can come closest to happiness or at least avoid misery.

SIGMUND FREUD

I was never much good at domestic work . . . My mother had a theory that if you didn't know how to do it you wouldn't have to.

MURIEL SPARK

❧

Wifedom with its connotations of monogamy, fidelity, possessiveness and jealousy is something that the liberated woman should do her best to avoid.

SIMONE DE BEAUVOIR

❧

To a certain extent all normal people sometimes wished their loved ones were dead.

ALBERT CAMUS

❧

Children embody all the elements of sacrifice, compromise, love and despair that are inherent in any marriage, yet the numerous small rewards they bring ultimately outweigh all discord they create.

CAROLINE BAILEY

❧

Life is only lived full time by women with children.

MARGUERITE DURAS

I enjoy solitude because I know there is a family awaiting my return.

ARNOLD WESKER

How any woman with a family ever put pen to paper I cannot fathom. Always the bell rings and the baker calls.

NIGEL NICOLSON

The universal instinct of family disparagement.

SOURCE UNKNOWN

So may families long continue to eat Friday night meals, Sunday lunches, wedding breakfasts and Christmas dinners, and may there always be cake in the house.

JEANETTE KUPFERMAN

The family, and no other conceivable structure, is the basic institution of society.

BRIGITTE BERGER

❦

There's only two things that last – your work and your family. It's what you have to show for how you lived.

JULIA SZABO

❦

Treasure your families: the future of humanity passes by the way of the families.

POPE JOHN PAUL II

❦

Oblovsky, like all unfaithful husbands, indeed, was very solicitous for his wife's comfort.

LEO TOLSTOY

❦

The demand for love is always absolute, based on the unappeasable original lack, and desire is not desire for this or that, but desire tout court. So that the reciprocation of love becomes 'giving what one does not have', a response produced from the 'realm of non-knowledge'.

JACQUES LACAN

A mother should not mistake her son's stomach for his heart.

SOURCE UNKNOWN

❧

. . . my daughter and granddaughter keep making these babies and expect me to take care of them. I ain't no nursemaid: I ain't old: and I ain't dead yet.

BETTY FRIEDAN

Only in the family are the individual's social tendencies aroused and developed and with these the capacity to take on responsibility for others. A person who has developed no family bonds will have a very hard time developing any larger loyalties in later life.

BRIGITTE BERGER

. . . the family is the suppressed home of all the virtues, where innocent children are tortured into their first falsehoods, where wills are broken by parental tyranny and self respect smothered by jostling egos.

AUGUST STRINDBERG

❧

. . . the mere necessity of sitting down in a dining-room at fixed hours fills my soul with a feeling of wretchedness. But when I participate in it (in practical life), when I sit down (at table), I know how to behave like anyone else.

GUSTAVE FLAUBERT

❧

While living our parents are the barriers between us and mortality. When they pass on we step up to the head of the line.

SOURCE UNKNOWN

❧

Looking at the mother, you might hope that the daughter would become like her, which is a prospective advantage equal to a dowry – the mother too often standing behind the daughter like a malignant prophecy – 'Such as I am, she will shortly be.'

GEORGE ELIOT

Other people's lovers are never comprehensible.

SIMONE DE BEAUVOIR

The men got angrier and angrier as their wives over the years got more confident and began to do more things instead of just taking care of them. The wives began to resent their husbands' demands on them. The men simply got more and more depressed. The women had crossed over to new roles, the men had not.

BETTY FRIEDAN

Christenings, weddings and funerals . . . are to life what breakfast, lunch and dinner are to the day. They break up the time and make people think they are doing something – but I'd just as soon make do with a packed lunch.

ALICE THOMAS ELLIS

It is a truth universally acknowledged, that a single man in possession of a good fortune, must be in want of a wife.

JANE AUSTEN

❧

Our marriage was bristling with tensions, but it was still a marriage. It was sustained by love which I do not have to define.

ANTHONY BURGESS

❧

You may argue that the working woman can ignore the lunch of the retired husband, or get him to make it himself, but such arguments do not allow for love and goodwill.

A. S. BYATT

On Love, Marriage and Family

She [Vita Sackville-West] is not an easy wife in the conventional way. She is a difficult wife. Yet she is everything on earth to me as you know . . . because although we have many tastes that are different, many activities that we do not share, essentially she and I are one.

HAROLD NICOLSON

❦

So often when husbands are trumpeting, one wonders what the silent wife is really thinking.

GERMAINE GREER

❦

A first-class wife and a second-class brain will defeat first-class brains and a second-class wife.

SOURCE UNKNOWN

❦

A good marriage puts us in touch with the transcendental.

JACK DOMINION

❦

My husband had given me the idea that I should die the second I escaped from him. Instead life became unbelievably exciting.

ANDRÉE PUTMAN

Those who attack marriage for its imperfections fail to notice that they are measuring it by the wrong yardstick. We should not measure any human institution against perfection, but against available alternatives.

HANS EYSENCK

❧

. . . nothing in this world was more difficult than love.

GABRIEL GARCÍA MÁRQUEZ

❧

A marriage where there are no arguments or fights is a dead marriage.

SOURCE UNKNOWN

On Love, Marriage and Family

Personally, I have not really suffered from it all that much. I've escaped most of the usual kinds of female slave labour, I have never been a mother or a housewife.

SIMONE DE BEAUVOIR

❧

Type A people can learn to speak kindly to their families, leave their watches at home and *smile*. They should look at plants, sit over their dinner table and read long, slow books: calming, classic, endless books that reduce this tempo to the personal best of an aged tortoise walking through the long grass.

MILTON FRIEDMAN

❧

Mere passion is only the beginning of love. People who don't have children and don't go through troubles together can't really love. So they move like bees from one appetite to another.

MALCOLM MUGGERIDGE

❧

In the welter of literature about marriage, one aspect of being married seems rarely to be mentioned, and that is space . . . Space is a significant factor in living together and creating a home.

CAROLINE BAILEY

In heterosexual love there's no solution. Man and woman are irreconcilable.

MARGUERITE DURAS

❧

A mother's job is to be there when her children need her, but to bring them up so that they don't.

SOURCE UNKNOWN

❧

. . . it is a pleasure of grandparents to spoil their grandchildren. They avenge themselves in that way on their children for the insults they have suffered from them.

CYRIL CONNOLLY

❧

Marriage is friendship: it's having someone you can always talk to and tell everything to and share everything with.

SIR JOHN MORTIMER

❧

. . . more than twenty-six years spent on constructing a mythology, a joint memory bank, a language, a signalling system of grunt and touch; all gone to waste… The end of a marriage is the end of civilization.

ANTHONY BURGESS

On Love, Marriage and Family

By far the most important channel of transmission of culture remains the family: and when family life fails to play its part, we must expect our culture to deteriorate.

T. S. ELIOT

Marriage should be a partnership – not an absorption by the greater or the less; not one part active and the other passive; one giving, the other receiving; one maintaining, the other maintained; none of these, but instead a perfect partnering, a perfect equality that should be equality of place, equality of privilege, equality of duty, equality of freedom.

RADCLYFFE HALL

Three different types of marriage. One for young people who just want to live together and have sex . . . another for couples who want to raise children. A third is for older people who want companionship.

MARGARET MEADE

. . . people have been encouraged to believe in the possibility of finding the 'right' person and the ideal relationship . . . But even the closest relationship is bound to have flaws and disadvantages . . .

ANTHONY STORR

❧

Our family is totally secular, but the Sabbath still holds a special meaning of family communion.

SOURCE UNKNOWN

❧

My number one passion was the adventures of love, the endless variations and tensions peculiar to the relations between the sexes.

ISAAC BASHEVIS SINGER

❧

Happiness is a usurer: for the loan of fifteen minutes of love it makes you pay with a whole cargo of misery.

GUSTAVE FLAUBERT

❧

Some men know how to make love to a woman and some men don't: that's all there is to it.

ANGUS WILSON

You have first claim on my love, but not on my time.

SIR PETER MEDAWAR

❧

It is an undoubted fact that all remarkable men have had remarkable mothers, and have respected them in after life as their best friends.

CHARLES DICKENS

There are two sorts of love – a self and an unselfish one. The first seeks to make the beloved minister to one's own good: the second seeks the good of the beloved before all else.

DERVLA MURPHY

❧

No family can hang out the sign: 'Nothing the matter here.'

CHINESE PROVERB

. . . the four great, intrinsic, inescapable upheavals that define the human condition – romantic love, being born, having children and dying.

MONTAIGNE

Marriage is a dangerous relationship, full of potential destruction of personality. People aren't meant to be together twenty-four hours a day.

MARGARET DRABBLE

All happy families resemble one another, each unhappy family is unhappy in its own way.

LEO TOLSTOY

Every monkey is a gazelle to its mother.

ARABIC SAYING

On Love, Marriage and Family

To deny one's being as a woman that has through the ages, been expressed in motherhood, nurturing, loving softness and tiger strength, is to deny one's personhood as a woman.

BETTY FRIEDAN

Every mother is a working woman.

SOURCE UNKNOWN

. . . women must realize that in making a commitment to a man, they have merged in his unconscious life with his mother and have therefore inherited the ambivalence with that relation.

CAMILLE PAGLIA

There was never any argument about the deeper value of our marriage, which could be viewed as a miniature civilization or micropolis . . . There was a fund of common memories to draw on, a series of codes, a potent, shorthand.

ANTHONY BURGESS

And like to runners hand the lamp of life One to another.

LUCRETIUS

A shared domestic life can offer a defence against the anxieties of everyday living.

CAROLINE BAILEY

❦

. . . There can't be more than one centre to a marriage. And if the man isn't the centre, it's an unhappy marriage.

STORM JAMESON

❦

Harold [Nicolson] stressed that marriage was a living organism 'a plant and not a piece of furniture. It grows; it changes; it develops.'

VITA SACKVILLE-WEST

❦

The happiest marriages are full of alternative lives, lived in the head, unknown to the partner.

SIR JOHN MORTIMER

❦

. . . when the husband walks back from the altar, he has already swallowed the choicest dainties of his bouquet. The beef and pudding of married life are then in store for him — or perhaps only the bread and cheese.

GEORGE ELIOT

Women are beaten by husbands who are judges or presiding magistrates as well as by husbands who are labourers.

SIMONE DE BEAUVOIR

❦

Multi-generational gatherings are the best history lesson the national curriculum can never provide.

SOURCE UNKNOWN

❦

There is no more sombre enemy of good art than the pram in the hall.

CYRIL CONNOLLY

He was a perfect husband: he never picked anything up from the floor, or turned out a light, or closed a door.

GABRIEL GARCÍA MÁRQUEZ

To live, as well as to die, a Jewish father needs to know that the future of his child is secure.

SIGMUND FREUD

In an ideal relationship both partners know they can live perfectly well without each other, but they also know they much prefer to live with each other.

KAREN HORNEY

Two opposing drives operate throughout life: the drive for companionship, love and everything else which brings use close to our fellow men; and the drive towards being separate, independent, autonomous.

ANTHONY STORR

... having children altered the whole texture and reality, changed the shape of the world ...

NORA BARTLETT

We may 'carve out' careers for ourselves, but our parentage gave us the implements with which to do it.

A. A. MILNE

✧

... Why is it just as we begin to go they begin to arrive, the fold in my neck clarifying as the fine bones of her hips sharpen? ...

SHARON OLDS

✧

Love is like scarlet fever — one has to go through it and get it over. They ought to find a way of being inoculated against love, like being vaccinated for smallpox.

LEO TOLSTOY

✧

Oh, every ungrateful child has a list of ways in which their parents failed them ...

JOSEPHINE HART

✧

The bond that physical happiness brings into being between a man and a woman is something whose importance I tend to underestimate.

SIMONE DE BEAUVOIR

The fact is simply that a child is a nuisance to a grown-up person. What is more, the nuisance becomes more and more intolerable as the grown-up person becomes more cultivated, more sensitive, and more engaged in the highest methods of adult work.

GEORGE BERNARD SHAW

The family should be recognized as the most stable and effective structure, not only for taking care of children but for meeting the needs of the sick and the handicapped and the aged.

BRIGITTE BERGER

Kafka and Proust never freed themselves from the expectations of their parents.

SOURCE UNKNOWN

On Life and Death

The fountain of contentment must spring up in the mind; and he who has so little knowledge of human nature as to seek happiness by changing anything but his own disposition will waste his life in fruitless efforts and multiply the griefs which he purposes to remove.

SAMUEL JOHNSON

The utility of living consists not in the length of days, but in the use of time; a man may have lived long, and yet lived but little.

MONTAIGNE

'What is the meaning of life . . . ?' Olga Knipper asks Chekhov. He replied, 'It is like asking what a carrot is. A carrot is a carrot and nothing more is known.'

ANTON CHEKHOV

It's better to have an unkempt flat than an unlived life.

ROSE MACCAULAY

Look to your health; and if you have it, praise God and value it next to a good conscience, for health is the second blessing that we mortals are capable of; a blessing that money cannot buy.

IZAAK WALTON

❧

Life is in the distractions.

SOURCE UNKNOWN

❧

I live like a plant, suffusing myself with sun and light, with colours and fresh air. I keep eating, so to speak; afterwards the digesting will have to be done, then the shitting; and the shit had better be good! That's the important thing.

GUSTAVE FLAUBERT

❧

Ah! Quand refleuriront les roses de Septembre?

PAUL VERLAINE

❧

There is no antidote against the opium of time . . . generations pass while some trees stand, and old families last not three oaks.

SIR THOMAS BROWNE

On Life and Death

Do not look too far ahead. Ahead there were the horrors
of death and farewells: it was false teeth, sciatica, infirmity,
intellectual barrenness, loneliness in a strange world that we
could no longer understand and that would carry on without
us . . . we have no choice in the matter.

SIMONE DE BEAUVOIR

J'aime le luxe, et même la mollesse.

VOLTAIRE

'The childhood years are the best years of your life . . .'
Whoever coined that was an unmitigated fuckwit, a bullshit
artist supreme. Life gets better the older you grow, until you
grow too old of course.

KERI HULME

Man is the only creature who can see his own death coming
. . . in old age there is a tendency . . . to be less involved in
life's dramas, more concerned with life's patterns.

ANTHONY STORR

I am delirious because I am dying so fast.

HENRY MILLER

Death is but an end to dying.

MONTAIGNE

No man is more frail than another,
No man more certain of tomorrow.

SENECA

On Life and Death

It seems to me one of the great sadnesses is that all of us understand tragedy to a certain extent, or sense it in our lives; loved things disappear, people you love die. But it's the comic side that some people can't see.

SOURCE UNKNOWN

❧

... Since while we are, death is not yet here; but when death is here we are no more – death does not concern us.

EPICURUS

❧

'There's not much in dying,' she thought. 'I shall go to sleep, and it will all be over.'

GUSTAVE FLAUBERT

❧

Old men must die; or the world would grow moldy, would only breed the past again.

ALFRED, LORD TENNYSON

❧

We must remember the old, the sick, the disabled and the dying and not let them be pushed to the margins of humanity.

POPE JOHN PAUL II

No man can stare too long at death or the sun.

LA ROCHEFOUCAULD

❧

Tell them I've had a wonderful life.

WITTGENSTEIN

❧

What is philosophy? It is the study of how to live contentedly and how to die peacefully.

SOURCE UNKNOWN

❧

Every man bears his death within himself, as the fruit bears the stone.

RILKE

❧

Life always fell short of dreams.

SIMONE DE BEAUVOIR

❧

Our life, what is it but a succession of preludes to that unknown aria whose first solemn note is sounded only by death?

FRANZ LISZT

Rage, rage, against the dying of the light.

DYLAN THOMAS

❧

I want Death to find me planting my cabbages, neither worrying about it nor the unfinished gardening.

MONTAIGNE

It matters not how a man dies, but how he lives.

SAMUEL JOHNSON

❧

Death is no different whined at than withstood.

PHILIP LARKIN

❧

And then one or other dies. And we think of this as love cut short; like a dance stopped in mid career or a flower with its head unluckily snapped off . . .

C. S. LEWIS

My mother's death was a beautiful experience for me. Death only had to smile at her and take her by the hand.

JEAN COCTEAU

❧

One doctor to another: 'About the termination of pregnancy – I want your opinion. The father was syphilitic. The mother tuberculous. Of the children born the first was blind, the second died, the third was deaf and dumb, the fourth was tuberculous. What would you have done?' 'I would have ended the next pregnancy.' 'Then you would have murdered Beethoven.'

MAURICE BARING

❧

He didn't want, when it came to die, to discover he hadn't lived.

HENRY DAVID THOREAU

❧

Longtemps, je me suis couché de bonne heure.

MARCEL PROUST

❧

Keep one thing in life and forget everything else.

HERBERT VON KARAJAN

[206]

To own a bit of ground, to scratch it with a hoe, to plant seeds, and watch their renewal of life – this is the commonest delight of the race, the most satisfactory thing a man can do.

CHARLES DUDLEY WARNER

❧

Life consists of a handful of joys soon scattered by indelible sorrows: but don't tell the children.

SOURCE UNKNOWN

❧

. . . I have come to believe that there can be no adequate preparation for the sadness that comes at the end, the sheer regret that one's life is finished, that one's failures remain indelible and one's successes illusory.

ANITA BROOKNER

Solitude offers a double advantage to the thinker: the first in being with himself, the second in not being with others.

VOLTAIRE

❧

You will never be happy if you continue to search for what happiness consists of. You will never live if you are looking for the meaning of life.

ALBERT CAMUS

❧

It is simply not true that works . . . depicting . . . imaginary human beings directly extend our knowledge of life. Direct knowledge of life is knowledge directly in relation to ourselves, it is our knowledge of how people behave in general, of what they are like in general, in so far as that part of life in which we ourselves have participated gives us material for generalization.

T. S. ELIOT

❧

Putting things off is the biggest waste of life: it snatches away each day as it comes, and denies us the present by promising the future. The greatest obstacle to living is expectancy, which hangs upon tomorrow and loses today.

SENECA

. . . with very few exceptions life ceases for us just when we are getting ready for it.

SENECA

Without music life would be a mistake.

FRIEDRICH NIETZSCHE

I am no more puzzled by the darkness into which I am going than by the darkness from which I came.

DAVID HUME

Consider whether this is a man
Who labours in the mud
Who knows no peace
Who fights for a crust of bread
Who dies at a yes or a no.

PRIMO LEVI

If you participate actively in life you don't see it clearly.

GUSTAVE FLAUBERT

❧

The secret of life is to have a task, something you devote your entire life to, something you bring everything to, every minute of the day for your whole life. And the most important thing is, it must be something you cannot possibly do.

HENRY MOORE

❧

A thing is not necessarily true because man dies for it.

OSCAR WILDE

❧

The Quality of daily life is what matters, the taste of the food on the table, the light in the room, the peace and wholeness of the moment.

GERMAINE GREER

❧

Your death is a part of the order of the Universe, 'tis a part of the life of the world . . . 'tis the condition of your creation . . . Give place to others as others have given place to you.

MONTAIGNE

On Life and Death

Growing old is a bore, but it's the only way to live a long time.

SOURCE UNKNOWN

❦

. . . So I learned that even after a single day's experience of the outside world a man could easily live a hundred years in prison. He'd have laid up enough memories never to be bored.

ALBERT CAMUS

❦

. . . If a man cannot enjoy his own company, what effect does he think it has on others? I am least lonely when I am alone in the hills and free to indulge my imagination; most lonely in a crowd.

A. WAINWRIGHT

Our life is frittered away by detail – simplify, simplify.

HENRY DAVID THOREAU

❧

I don't know any other way to succeed in life other than by extremely hard work.

ALBERT ROUX

❧

One of the great ironies of modern life is that many people have little idea of how to spend the increased leisure time . . . it is sad that people often . . . speak in terms of 'killing time' and of 'passing time', for time should be man's most precious possession.

RABBI JULIAN JACOBS

❧

Young folks may get fond of each other before they know what life is, and they may think it all holiday if they can only get together; but it soon turns into a working day, my dear.

GEORGE ELIOT

❧

Given that you've got to die, it obviously doesn't matter exactly how or when.

ALBERT CAMUS

On Life and Death

A man, his destiny, and his work – are one.

PHILIP ROTH

❦

Habit is the denial of creativity and the negation of freedom; a self-imposed strait-jacket of which the wearer is unaware.

ARTHUR KOESTLER

❦

You've had a good innings. It's time to hang up your bat.

CLEMENT ATTLEE

Les beaux jours sont finis, la fin de ma vie n'est pas drôle.

GUSTAVE FLAUBERT

❦

. . . Those who fear life are already three parts dead.

BERTRAND RUSSELL

❦

One doesn't soon learn the trade of life.

HENRY DAVID THOREAU

Culture may even be described simply as that which makes life worth living.

T. S. ELIOT

⚜

The Grave's a fine and private place, but none I think do there embrace.

ANDREW MARVELL

⚜

The intellect of man is forced to choose
Perfection of the life, or of the work.

W. B. YEATS

⚜

Suffering is the most real mode of life, the one for which we are all ultimately created.

OSCAR WILDE

Style is an attitude to life and living . . . it is a concern for other people, making them feel loved, introducing them, making everything look marvellous . . .

SIR ROY STRONG

❧

The more one lives the more one suffers.

GUSTAVE FLAUBERT

❧

While the hemlock was being prepared, Socrates was learning a melody on the flute. 'What use will that be to you?' he was asked. 'At least I will learn this melody before I die.'

❧

. . . you must not think that a man has lived long because he has white hair and wrinkles: he has not lived long, just existed long.

SENECA

❧

It cannot be supposed that nature, often having wisely distributed to all the previous periods of life their peculiar and proper enjoyments, should have neglected . . . the last act of the human drama, and left it destitute of suitable advantages.

CICERO

Death does not concern us because as long as we exist death is not here. And when it does come we no longer exist.

EPICURUS

❧

Live all you can; it's a mistake not to.

HENRY JAMES

❧

Destiny stands by sarcastic with our dramatis personae folded in her hand.

GEORGE ELIOT

❧

I cannot interest myself in anything that is not life.

COLETTE

Life is full of conflict and satisfaction in living can only be gained by coming to terms with the difficulties.

SOURCE UNKNOWN

❧

It is questionable if all the mechanical inventions yet made have lightened the day's toil of any human being!

JOHN STUART MILL

❧

The burden of existence doesn't weigh on our shoulders while we are composing.

GUSTAVE FLAUBERT

❧

The unexamined life is not worth living.

SOCRATES

❧

It is a long time since I ceased to exist. I merely fill the place of someone they take for me.

ANDRÉ GIDE

❧

The mass of men lead lives of quiet desperation.

HENRY DAVID THOREAU

Life is either too empty or too full.

VIRGINIA WOOLF

❧

He has not learnt the lesson of life who does not every day surmount a fear.

RALPH WALDO EMERSON

❧

I see life more as an affair of solitude diversified by company than as an affair of company diversified by solitude.

PHILIP LARKIN

One must have a decisive attitude to life. This is a pre-requisite for growth.

SOURCE UNKNOWN

❧

We shall find life tolerable once we have consented to be always ill at ease.

GUSTAVE FLAUBERT

On Life and Death

In extreme old age other people, and frequently old people themselves, usually think that they are only living out their days . . . it is in extremely old age that the most valuable and necessary life both for oneself and others is lived. The value of life is in inverse proportion to the square of the distance from death.

ERICA JONG

Say this when you mourn for me:
There was a man — and look, he is no more.
He died before his time.
The music of his life suddenly stopped.
A pity! There was another song in him.
Now it is lost
Forever.

CHAIM NACHMAN BIALIK

On Random Thoughts

A boor cannot be sin-fearing, nor can an ignorant man be pious.

RABBI HILLEL

Were I to hold the truth in my hand I would let it go for the positive joy of seeking.

RALPH WALDO EMERSON

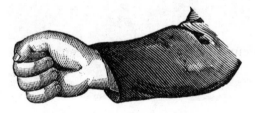

If I could see further than others — it is because I stood on the shoulders of giants.

SIR ISAAC NEWTON

In the country I always fear that creation will expire before tea-time.

REV. SYDNEY SMITH

On Random Thoughts

Ask a toad what is beauty and he will reply, 'a female toad with two great round eyes, a large flat mount and a brown back'.

VOLTAIRE

❦

Because you are born in a stable you are not necessarily a horse.

DUKE OF WELLINGTON

❦

The circus doesn't creep into town.

STUBBY KAYE

❦

When prejudices fade away human beings come to see each other.

SOURCE UNKNOWN

❦

Supposing no one played tennis because they wouldn't make Wimbledon?

PHILIP LARKIN

❦

You don't have to be a chef to judge an omelette.

SOURCE UNKNOWN

Always dream and shoot higher than you know you can do
. . . Try to be better than yourself.

WILLIAM FAULKNER

༚

Some of the greatest creators were people of depressive
temperament. Michelangelo, Robert Schumann, Balzac,
Virginia Woolf, John Stuart Mill and Winston Churchill.

ANTHONY STORR

༚

The principle of procrastinated rape is said to be the ruling
one in all the great bestsellers.

V. S. PRITCHETT

༚

There are no facts, only interpretations.

FRIEDRICH NIETZSCHE

༚

It is never too late to give up our prejudices.

HENRY DAVID THOREAU

༚

Sentiment is unearned emotion.

SOURCE UNKNOWN

On Random Thoughts

Never be happy-go-lucky in remembering the gratitude you owe to others.

SOURCE UNKNOWN

You would not have sought me unless you had already found me.

BLAISE PASCAL

This is an important book, the critic assumes, because it deals with war. This is an insignificant book, because it deals with the feelings of women in a drawing room.

VIRGINIA WOOLF

It is better to light a candle than curse the darkness.

CHINESE PROVERB

There is a power that works within us without consulting us.

VOLTAIRE

Those who cannot remember the past are condemned to repeat it.

SANTAYANA

❧

Great talent takes place in the everyday.

SAUL BELLOW

❧

If your train's on the wrong track, every station you come to is the wrong station.

BERNARD MALAMUD

Literature no longer has the appeal it had when I was young, when people were bought up to read books and there was no competition with other kinds of entertainment.

SOURCE UNKNOWN

On Random Thoughts

Words that do not come from the heart do not enter the ear.

MOSHE BEN EZRA

❧

Make decisions quickly. It is better to make occasional mistakes than to stagnate.

PETER BULOS

❧

I don't want it good, I want it Tuesday.

JACK WARNER

❧

I have no relish for the country. It is a kind of healthy grave.

REV. SYDNEY SMITH

❧

It is not the place which brings honour to the man, but the man who brings honour to the place.

RABBI YOSI

❧

If a man does not keep pace with his companions, perhaps it is because he hears a different drummer. Let him step to the music which he hears, however measured or far away.

HENRY DAVID THOREAU

Today is the first day of the rest of your life. Make the best of it.

SIR BERNARD BRAINE

❧

When thou hast done, thou hast not done, for I have more.

JOHN DONNE

❧

. . . contemplation would seem to be the only activity that is appreciated for its own sake . . . nothing is gained from it except the act of contemplation . . .

ARISTOTLE

❧

One thing only I know and that is that I know nothing.

SOCRATES

❧

Never break an engagement no matter how trivial.

PETER BULOS

❧

Start every journey ten minutes early. Not only will you avoid the stress of haste, but if all goes well you'll have ten minutes to relax before your next engagement.

PAUL WILSON

On Random Thoughts

To walk alone in London is the greatest rest.

VIRGINIA WOOLF

❧

Songbirds do not study in a conservatory.

SAUL BELLOW

❧

Have nothing in your houses which you do not know to be useful or believe to be beautiful.

WILLIAM MORRIS

❧

Le signe distinctif d'une femme bien née, c'est de se connâitre en cuisine.

TALLEYRAND

If you have built castles in the air, your work need not be lost; that is where they should be. Now put the foundations under them.

HENRY DAVID THOREAU

He goes to parties and uneasily tries to disentangle envy from admiration, only to discover that even where the admiration is sincere, it is not for his book or his play, but for the success itself.

SOURCE UNKNOWN

On s'engage, puis on voit.

NAPOLEON BONAPARTE

Writers don't make good husbands. They reserve their Eros for their art.

SAUL BELLOW

On Random Thoughts

To sell a product you must inform the world of its existence.

ROGER SCRUTON

❧

Only dull people are brilliant at breakfast.

OSCAR WILDE

❧

The loud wheel gets the oil.

SOURCE UNKNOWN

❧

Do not judge your fellow man until you have been in his position.

RABBI HILLEL

❧

'Obscenity' is not a term capable of exact legal definition; in the practice of the courts, it means 'anything that shocks the magistrate'.

BERTRAND RUSSELL

❧

Where observation is concerned, chance favours only the prepared mind.

LOUIS PASTEUR

Don't let your opinions sway your judgement.

SAM GOLDWYN

❧

It is better to overrate than underrate yourself.

SOURCE UNKNOWN

❧

A joke is an epigram on the death of a feeling.

FRIEDRICH NIETZSCHE

❧

Work is preferable to almost all leisure.

SIR JOHN MORTIMER

❧

We must always have our boots on, and be ready to leave.

MONTAIGNE

❧

If you let the reins loose the horse will find its way home.

GRAHAM GREENE

❧

Nothing shall come of nothing.

WILLIAM SHAKESPEARE

We readily criticize the defects of others, but rarely take the opportunity to correct these defects in ourselves.

LA ROCHEFOUCAULD

❧

We ought to restrict ourselves, so far as possible, to the simple and natural, and not to magnify that which is little or belittle that which is great.

BLAISE PASCAL

Women have been condemned as castrating or domineering when they have attempted to assert their rights.

SUSIE ORBACH

❧

You can stop a quarrel before it starts.

SOURCE UNKNOWN

I do not like undertaking anything until I am physically as impeccable, as fully prepared, as I am psychologically.

SIMONE DE BEAUVOIR

❦

La verité consiste dans les nuances.

ERNEST RENAN

❦

Muddy waters let stand become clear.

LAO TSE

❦

Start nothing that you cannot finish.

MUSAR HAPHILOSOPHIM

❦

The original and classic psychoanalytic process cannot operate if the patient is mute or the analyst deaf.

GEORGE STEINER

❦

The house seems to take up so much time . . . when I have to clean up twice or wash up unnecessary things I get frightfully impatient and want to be working.

PAMELA HANSFORD JOHNSON

On Random Thoughts

. . . Meetings, parties, jubilees . . . People think they are occupied with various important matters but they are only occupied with gluttony.

LEO TOLSTOY

❧

City air makes us free. There is something energizing and liberating about city life.

SOURCE UNKNOWN

❧

A foolish consistency is the hobgoblin of little minds.

RALPH WALDO EMERSON

❧

Birds do not make good ornithologists.

BARNETT NEWMAN

The more we face our own conflicts and seek out our own solutions, the more inner freedom and strength we will gain.

KAREN HORNEY

❧

If you live to be ninety in England and can still eat a boiled egg, they think you deserve the Nobel Prize.

ALAN BENNETT

❧

Nothing has been learned; Auschwitz has not even served as a warning. For more detailed information, consult your daily newspaper.

ELIE WIESEL

The possession of a camera can inspire something akin to lust. And like all credible forms of lust, it cannot be satisfied: first, where the possibilities of photography are infinite; and second, because the project is finally self-devouring.

SUSAN SONTAG

On Random Thoughts

We have terms like 'sexual harassment' and 'battered women'. A few years ago, they were just called 'life'.

GLORIA STEINEM

❦

You need a magnetic field of concentration round you, no matter how sympathetic you are to the other person's work.

SOURCE UNKNOWN

❦

. . . the *oublieuse mémoire*, the memory that forgets because it selects, and, by its selection creates.

COLETTE

❦

The *légion d'honneur* seems to me a reward that's given to the mediocrities wholesale.

SIMONE DE BEAUVOIR

❦

A great mind must be androgynous.

SAMUEL TAYLOR COLERIDGE

❦

You destroy my solitude without providing me with company.

MARIE DE RABUTIN-CHANTAL, MARQUISE DE SÉVIGNÉ

Most creative people long for structure to their lives. They long to be told that they have to do something by breakfast tomorrow.

SOURCE UNKNOWN

❦

Almost all great monuments of the past have added in one way or another to the misery of mankind, either through use of sweated labour or through inflation caused by prodigal spending.

JEAN GIMPEL

❦

He will hold thee, when his passion shall have spent its novel force, something better than his dog, a little dearer than his horse.

ALFRED, LORD TENNYSON

On Random Thoughts

. . . she [Vita Sackville-West] longed for new places, for movement, for places 'where no one will want me to order lunch or pay housebooks'.

HAROLD NICOLSON

❧

Never again to be forced to move to the rhythm of others.

TILLIE OLSEN

❧

Years of actually getting up in front of audiences have taught me only three lessons.

One: you don't die. Two: there's no *right* way to speak – only your way. Three: it's worth it.

GLORIA STEINEM

❧

Assertiveness is *not* aggressiveness . . .

SOURCE UNKNOWN

❧

Pragmatically, aesthetic value can be recognized or experienced, but it cannot be conveyed to those who are incapable of grasping its sensations and perceptions. To quarrel on its behalf is always a blunder.

HAROLD BLOOM

Give all thou canst, high Heaven rejects the lore.
Of nicely-calculated less or more.

WILLIAM WORDSWORTH

❧

What mattered about talking . . . was not only what the
patient says, but who he or she says it to.

SIGMUND FREUD

❧

. . . salvias are the sure sign of the wrong sort of gardener —
maximum effort to minimal style, when it should be the
other way round.

KATHARINE WHITEHORN

❧

Women were powered by their years, by their babies, by their
passage on the planet; men grew oddly depleted. So a woman
of thirty-nine and a man of twenty-five met at an equal point
sexually. This was the great truth French novelists knew . . .

ERICA JONG

❧

One of the paradoxes of escaping is that if you do it too often
it becomes routine and no escape.

SOURCE UNKNOWN

On Random Thoughts

Il faut du temps pour etre femme.

SOURCE UNKNOWN

❧

Read not the Times, read the Eternities.

HENRY DAVID THOREAU

❧

I should never call myself a book lover any more than a people lover. It all depends what's inside them.

PHILIP LARKIN

During the interval between dinner and the arrival of the guests, Kitty felt as a young soldier feels before going into action. Her heart throbbed violently and she could not keep her thoughts fixed on anything.

LEO TOLSTOY

Nothing is written in marble or in stone.

SOURCE UNKNOWN

Nature has given women so much power that the law has wisely given them little.

SAMUEL JOHNSON

If anything vexed her, it was the perpetual chore of daily meals. For they not only had to be served on time: they had to be perfect, and they had to be just what he wanted to eat, without his having to be asked.

GABRIEL GARCÍA MÁRQUEZ

Quantitatively, there is every reason to believe that we speak inside and to ourselves more than we speak outward and to anyone else.

GEORGE STEINER

On Random Thoughts

*Les traductions sont comme les femmes; quand elles sont belles, elles
ne sont pas fidèles, et quand elles sont fidèles, elles ne sont pas belles.*

SOURCE UNKNOWN

❦

In a crowded boat, one man begins to dig a hole in the wood
under him and when challenged, replies that it is his own
affair, it is his own part of the boat that he is boring.

RABBI SIMEON BAR YOHAI

❦

Levin did not like talking and hearing about the beauty of
nature . . . words for him detracted from the beauty of what
he saw.

LEO TOLSTOY

❦

> I have spread my dreams under your feet;
> Tread softly for you tread on my dreams.

W. B. YEATS

❦

. . . in an effort to love and understand women . . . he looked
to them to love and understand *him*, and it occurred to him
that this was true of most men.

ANITA BROOKNER

They [men] can build houses, but they can't make homes.

MARGUERITE DURAS

❧

Invalids make me depressed and angry, children irritate me.

COLETTE

❧

The pleasures of high society are no pleasure at all for a happy woman.

STENDHAL

❧

Thought little. It's impossible in company . . . I prefer to be alone. But I am not alone when Sonya is with me.

LEO TOLSTOY

❧

He [Anthony Trollope] knew nothing about plants, and grew bored when being conducted round botanical gardens . . .

VICTORIA GLENDINNING

❧

Whatever home one was raised in, that was the faith one accepted.

ISAAC BASHEVIS SINGER

The *lecture* is an instrument for the bourgeoisie . . .

MARCEL PROUST

❧

Choosing and appearing in new clothes made her [Virginia Woolf] rigid with fear and embarrassment.

SOURCE UNKNOWN

❧

Everything is accepted in Bohemia except non-conformity.

DAVID MAMET

. . . all a woman needs is a black skirt, a pair of black pants, a black sweater and a raincoat.

YVES SAINT LAURENT

❧

Good and evil coexist without the one influencing the other.

ELIE WIESEL

. . . men have to have an opinion. I only have opinions on things I know something about. Men aren't like that at all. They have opinions.

MARGARET DRABBLE

๛

'Thinking what to eat' is an endless duty, however creative the actual task may be. This one latent function of the creative cookery ideal is the product of dissatisfaction.

CHRISTOPHER DRIVER

Who will breast *The Waves* when Mrs Woolf's diaries and letters are all now at hand like a life-preserver.

GORE VIDAL

๛

I myself tend to be apolitical and have difficulty even comprehending the vocabulary of politics.

OLIVER SACKS

On Random Thoughts

The only meaning of technique is clarity.

DAVID MAMET

❧

Nagging is an expression of powerlessness. If nags had power they wouldn't have to nag.

SOURCE UNKNOWN

❧

Men are the egotists of life of course. Women are the conformists. And again, men need to advertise comradeship and ease, women are content to feel it.

ANGUS WILSON

❧

During the day I try not to speak too much because it interrupts the rhythm of the sentences.

SHERE HITE

❧

Memory? How often people take memory for intelligence. And they don't see that memory excludes intelligence, is incompatible with intelligence – intelligence which solves problem in an original manner. The one is a substitute for the other.

LEO TOLSTOY

Once you stop hunting, something in the male dies.

ROD STEIGER

❧

Commonplaces are put to use only by imbeciles or geniuses. Mediocre natures avoid them; they seek out the exceptional, the highs and lows.

MARIO VARGOS LLOSA

❧

Sex illuminates the day. It's not a thing for the night.

SOURCE UNKNOWN

Jardine . . . takes care of the house, the finances, the travel, the cooking, the shopping, the correspondence, the filing. She keeps the outside world at bay.

MURIEL SPARK

On Random Thoughts

It will finally be recognized that Hollywood was one of the great art centres of the world.

JEAN GIMPEL

❧

The present code of sexual explicitness may be related to the general malaise of the novel . . . Have we lost the curious wonder of an imagined living presence, the paradox of reality by which Anna Karenina or Isabel Archer outlive their begetters and will outlive us.

GEORGE STEINER

❧

Every reiteration of the idea that *nothing matters* debases the human spirit.

DAVID MAMET

❧

A Russian astronaut and a Russian brain surgeon were discussing religion. The brain surgeon was a Christian but the astronaut was not.

ASTRONAUT: 'I've been out in space many times, but I've never seen God or angels.'

BRAIN SURGEON: 'I've operated on many clever brains, but I've never seen a single thought.'

SOURCE UNKNOWN

I always fight against routine: I believe that a person should not have one day which is exactly like another; he loses the feeling that each day of life is God's gift.

MSTISLAV ROSTROPOVICH

❧

To speak and not punish. To speak and not condemn.
To speak in order to educate and enrich, not to repudiate and humiliate. To speak to cure, not to hurt and wound.

ELIE WIESEL

❧

Culture is one thing we cannot deliberately aim at. It is the product of a variety of more or less harmonious activities, each pursued for its own sake: the artist must concentrate upon his canvas, the poet upon his typewriter, the civil servant upon the just settlement of particular problems as they present themselves upon his desk.

T. S. ELIOT

❧

Reading *Mein Kampf* does not make a fascist. Reading the Bible does not make a Christian. Reading *Das Kapital* does not make a Marxist . . .

SOURCE UNKNOWN

The Scylla of plot and the Charybdis of total plotlessness.

SOURCE UNKNOWN

Being airborne in space generates a lot of ideas; so does staying at an hotel where the service is good.

CHRISTIAN LACROIX

Pacifism is a philosophy which, unfortunately, only appeals to pacifists.

ARTHUR KOESTLER

Those who think they know it all usually know the least; those who think they have all the answers have always lost the plot.

SIR JOHN MORTIMER

Index of Contributors

Abbado, Claudio 163

Ackroyd, Peter 25, 26, 42, 44

Aldiss, Brian 172

Amidon, Stephen 93

Amis, Sir Kingsley 149

Amis, Martin 26, 43, 63, 65

Appelfeld, Aharon 143, 158

Archer, Jeffrey 48

Aristotle 50, 117, 152, 226

Attlee, Clement 213

Atwood, Margaret 90

Auden, W. H. 65, 108, 114

Augustine, St 102

Austen, Jane 58, 148, 184

Ayer, A. J. 117

Bacon, Francis 60, 105, 109

Bailey, Caroline 142, 166, 167, 177, 178, 187, 194

Baring, Maurice 206

Barnes, Julian 26, 37, 39

Bartlett, Nora 196

Bayley, John 46

Beckett, Samuel 76

Beerbohm, Max 143

Beethoven, Ludwig van 159

Belloc, Hilaire 22

Bellow, Saul 25, 47, 78, 116, 136, 139, 224, 227, 228

Belshaw, Chris 169

Benchley, Robert 18

Bennett, Alan 234

Bennett, Arnold 97

Berger, Brigitte 176, 180, 181, 198

Berkoff, Steven 169

Berlin, Isaiah 102, 114

Bettelheim, Bruno 56

Bialik, Chaim Nachman 219

Blake, William 128

Blanch, Lesley 92

Blond, Anthony 35, 94

Bloom, Harold 45, 63, 237

Bonaparte, Napoleon 228

Boteach, Rabbi Shmuel 146

Botton, Alain de 47, 78, 100, 175

Bowen, Elizabeth 77

Boyd, William 151

Braine, Sir Bernard 226

Brenan, Gerald 38

Brome, Vincent 31

Brooke, Stopford A. 92

Brookner, Anita 16, 151, 154, 207, 241

Browne, Sir Thomas 200

Bruyère, La 65, 155

Bulos, Peter 162, 164, 166, 225, 226

Burgess, Anthony 35, 42, 59, 62, 70, 78, 85, 88, 100, 122, 138, 184, 188, 193

Burke, Edmund 164

Butler, Samuel 101, 122

Byatt, A. S. 184

Index of Contributors

Calvino, Italo 51

Campbell, Mrs Patrick 138

Campton, David 23, 26, 122, 142

Camus, Albert 118, 139, 141, 174, 178, 208, 211, 212

Capote, Truman 62

Carroll, Lewis 79

Cartland, Dame Barbara 123

Carver, Raymond 125

Caute, David 54

Cesarani, David 151

Chanel, Coco 168

Channing, William Ellery 83

Chekhov, Anton 35, 69, 199

Chesterfield, Earl of 95

Churchill, Sir Winston 60

Cicero 147, 215

Clarke, Jeremy 172

Cockerell, Sir Sydney 139

Cocteau, Jean 109, 206

Cohen, Sandra 81, 84

Coleridge, Samuel Taylor 235

Colette 82, 136, 216, 235, 242

Collins, Wilkie 139

Connolly, Cyril 188, 195

Conrad, Joseph 140

Coward, Noël 113, 145

Crichton, Michael 156

Day Lewis, Cecil 32

de Beauvoir, Simone 56, 82, 96, 101, 108, 129, 133, 136, 142, 166, 178, 183, 187, 195, 197, 201, 204, 232, 235

de Gaulle, Charles 136

de la Mare, Walter 110

De Quincey, Thomas 136

Drabble, Margaret 85, 192, 244

Delafield, E. M. 48

De Vries, Peter 38

Dickens, Charles 22, 40, 68, 71, 191

Dominion, Jack 185

Donne, John 226

Dostoyevsky, Fyodor 121

Driver, Christopher 244

Duras, Marguerite 75, 90, 145, 177, 178, 188, 242

Ecclesiastes, Book of 54

Eliot, George 64, 182, 194, 212, 216

Eliot, T. S. 13, 53, 97, 107, 147, 189, 208, 214, 248

Elliot, David 24, 94

Ellis, Alice Thomas 183

Elon, Amos 154

Emerson, Ralph Waldo 33, 58, 64, 152, 173, 218, 220, 233

Epicurus 203, 216

Estienne, Henri 164

Eysenck, Hans 186

Ezra, Moshe Ben 225

Faulkner, William 13, 18, 62, 222

Fielding, Helen 42

Flaubert, Gustave 27, 28, 32, 35, 38, 51, 53, 57, 59, 61, 66, 71, 75, 76, 78, 84, 88, 89, 91, 92, 94, 96, 99, 103, 107, 126, 129, 134, 161, 162, 172, 173, 182, 190, 200, 203, 210, 213, 215, 217, 218

Forster, E. M. 61, 77

Fowles, John 17, 37, 120, 162
France, Anatole 66, 103
Fraser, Helen 28
Freud, Sigmund 88, 129, 132, 157, 171, 174, 177, 196, 238
Friedan, Betty 176, 181, 183, 193
Friedman, Milton 187

Gandhi, Mahatma 160
García Márquez, Gabriel 14, 92, 186, 195, 240
Gauguin, Paul 113
Gebler, Carlo 70
Gellhorn, Martha 30
George V, King 104
Gerard, Jasper 44
Gertler, Mark 139
Gide, André 11, 68, 118, 217
Gimpel, Jean 34, 80, 126, 236, 247
Gissing, George 87, 142
Glendinning, Victoria 39, 46, 167, 242
Golding, William 15, 29, 52
Goldwyn, Sam 230
Gordimer, Nadine 13, 21
Gordon, Giles 47
Gove, Michael 89
Greene, Graham 25, 54, 63, 72, 75, 230
Greer, Germaine 102, 170, 185, 210

Hall, Radclyffe 189
Hansford Johnson, Pamela 232
Haphilosophim, Musar 232
Hardy, Robert 77
Hardy, Thomas 30

Hare, David 155
Hart, Josephine 197
Hazlitt, William 155
Hearn, Lafcadio 105
Heine, Heinrich 71, 91
Heller, Joseph 145
Hemingway, Ernest 19, 23, 32, 50, 66, 70, 78, 79, 90
Hesse, Hermann 153, 173
Hillel, Rabbi 131, 220, 229
Hird, Dame Thora 147
Hite, Shere 245
Hobbes, Thomas 172
Hodges, Jack 24
Holloway, David 82
Holroyd, Michael 118, 121
Horney, Karen 196, 234
Horowitz, Rabbi Isaiah 162
Hulme, Keri 201
Hume, David 209
Huxley, Aldous 133

Inge, William Ralph 57
Isaiah, Book of 6
Isherwood, Christopher 72

Jacobs, Rabbi Julian 104, 212
Jacobson, Howard 116
James, Henry 29, 58, 216
Jameson, Storm 194
Jerome, Jerome K. 43
John Paul II, Pope 180, 203
Johnson, Samuel 24, 27, 28, 98, 102, 140, 199, 205, 240

Index of Contributors

Jones, Ernest 114

Jong, Erica 20, 45, 49, 85, 111, 141, 165, 219, 238

Josipovici, Gabriel 32, 33

Kafka, Franz 20, 40, 145

Karajan, Herbert von 206

Karan, Donna 105

Kaye, Stubby 221

Keneally, Thomas 15

Kennedy, John F. 153

King, Francis 27, 130

Kingsley, Charles 147

Kissinger, Henry 147

Klima, Ivan 121

Koch, F. H. 50

Koestler, Arthur 50, 98, 99, 213, 249

Koestler, Cynthia 28

Kundera, Milan 36

Kupferman, Jeanette 179

Lacan, Jacques 180

Lacroix, Christian 249

Lang, Stephen 149

Lao Tse 232

Larkin, Philip 28, 68, 82, 83, 84, 131, 205, 218, 221, 239

Lear, Norman 19

Leavis, Q. D. 15, 39, 55

Lee, Hermione 14, 19

Leonardo da Vinci 101

Lessing, Doris 18, 44, 62, 64, 98, 101, 137, 148, 151

Levi, Primo 19, 135, 209

Levin, Bernard 31, 64, 102, 120, 122

Lewis, C. S. 205

Ligeti, György 115

Linklater, Eric 31

Liszt, Franz 204

Lively, Adam 84, 89

Lively, Penelope 66

Lodge, David 31, 61

Lucretius 193

MacCaulay, Rose 199

MacLeod, Alistair 72

Magee, William Connor 175

Maimonides 143, 163

Major, John 104

Malamud, Bernard 224

Mamet, David 40, 41, 45, 69, 86, 92, 93, 116, 119, 150, 243, 245, 247

Mandela, Nelson 163, 171

Mandelstam, Nadezhda 81, 160

Mann, Thomas 67

Marlow, Joyce 89

Marvell, Andrew 214

Masefield, John 72

Maugham, W. Somerset 20, 60, 95, 110, 117

Maupassant, Guy de 56

Maurois, André 156

Meade, Margaret 189

Medawar, Sir Peter 126, 191

Melville, Herman 16

Michener, James 108

Mill, John Stuart 145, 170, 217

Miller, Alice 141

Miller, Betty 156

Miller, Henry 38, 202

Miller, Jonathan 118
Milne, A. A. 197
Mizner, Wilson 80
Montaigne 6, 137, 147, 150, 153, 155, 157, 165,
    192, 199, 202, 205, 210, 230
Montesquieu 96, 161
Moore, Henry 115, 210
Morris, William 143, 227
Mortimer, Sir John 11, 23, 37, 74, 119, 155,
    188, 194, 230, 249
Mozart, Leopold 112
Mozart, Wolfgang Amadeus 99
Muggeridge, Malcolm 120, 187
Murphy, Dervla 158, 191
Murray, Jock 6, 138

Nabokov, Vladimir 26, 29, 35, 51, 52, 140
Naipaul, V. S. 47
Nell, Victor 88
Newman, Barnett 233
Newton, Sir Isaac 220
Nichols, Grace 43
Nicolson, Harold 129, 185, 237
Nicolson, Nigel 73, 179
Nietzsche, Friedrich 129, 146, 209, 222, 230
Nixon, Peter 130

Oates, Joyce Carol 70
O'Brien, Edna 12
O'Hanlon, Redmond 22
Olds, Sharon 197
Olsen, Tillie 237
Orbach, Susie 231
Ortega y Gasset, José 146

Orwell, George 67, 73, 144
Oz, Amos 40, 53, 157, 175
Ozick, Cynthia 21

Paglia, Camille 113, 193
Parker, Dorothy 60
Pascal, Blaise 48, 79, 223, 231
Pasteur, Louis 229
Picasso, Pablo 120, 144
Pizzey, Erin 161
Plater, Alan 86, 110, 140
Pollack, Sydney 46, 123
Potter, Beatrix 65
Pratchett, Terry 68
Priestley, J. B. 12, 83, 124, 134
Pritchett, V. S. 31, 41, 169, 222
Proust, Marcel 13, 97, 106, 111, 112, 113, 206,
    243
Putman, Andrée 185
Pym, Barbara 132
Pythagoras 144

Quiller-Couch, Arthur 108

Raphael, Frederick 127
Ray, Satyajit 125
Reich-Ranicki, Marcel 40
Renan, Ernest 232
Reynolds, Sir Joshua 167
Richler, Mordechai 119
Rilke 124, 204
Roberts, Kenneth 87
Rochefoucauld, La 133, 158, 204, 231
Rostropovich, Mstislav 248

Index of Contributors

Roth, Henry 44, 213

Roth, Philip 14, 33, 70, 135, 166, 172

Rousseau, Jean-Jacques 168

Roux, Albert 212

Ruskin, John 97

Russell, Bertrand 134, 213, 229

Sacks, Oliver 244

Sackville-West, Vita 131, 194

Sagan, Françoise 124, 130

Sainte-Beuve 18

Saint Laurent, Yves 243

Sand, George 106

Sartre, Jean-Paul 143

Santayana 224

Schnitzler, Arthur 129

Schopenhauer, Arthur 111, 153

Scruton, Roger 75, 148, 229

Segal, Clancy 12

Seneca 79, 154, 156, 158, 202, 208, 209, 215

Seth, Vikram 70, 87

Sévigné, Marie de Rabutin-Chantal, Marquise de 235

Seymour, Gerald 90

Shakespeare, William 133, 230

Shaw, George Bernard 84, 119, 198

Shaw, Sir Roy 101

Sibelius, Jean 113

Sillitoe, Alan 162

Simenon, Georges 20, 76, 81

Singer, Isaac Bashevis 16, 52, 56, 58, 63, 76, 95, 170, 173, 190, 242

Smith, Rev. Sydney 68, 220, 225

Snow, C. P. 80

Socrates 215, 217, 226

Solzhenitsyn, Alexander 103, 159

Sontag, Susan 78, 168, 234

Spark, Muriel 91, 116, 178, 246

Stassinopolous, Arianna 158

Steiger, Rod 246

Stein, Gertrude 107

Steinem, Gloria 17, 19, 56, 161, 235, 237

Steiner, George 34, 36, 55, 56, 83, 97, 98, 232, 240, 247

Stendhal 112, 140, 242

Sterne, Laurence 91

Stevenson, Adlai 85, 175

Stoppard, Tom 24

Storr, Anthony 14, 110, 115, 123, 125, 135, 164, 171, 190, 196, 202, 222

Strindberg, August 143, 182

Strong, Sir Roy 215

Strutt, Mike 169

Sutherland, Stuart 75

Szabo, Julia 180

Talleyrand 227

Tennyson, Alfred, Lord 203, 236

Teresa of Calcutta, Mother 161

Theroux, Paul 100

Thomas, D. M. 130

Thomas, Dylan 205

Thoreau, Henry David 170, 206, 212, 213, 217, 222, 225, 228, 239

Tolstoy, Leo 15, 38, 45, 109, 148, 174,177, 180, 192, 197, 233, 239, 241, 242, 245

Toynbee, Philip 148

Tremain, Rose 94

Trevelyan, G. M. 105
Trevor, William 24, 72
Trollope, Anthony 12, 36, 64, 72, 77, 91, 92
Trollope, Mrs 74
Tsvetayeva, Marina 169
Turgenev, Ivan 80
Twain, Mark 156
Tynan, Kenneth 118

Updike, John 15, 30, 34, 52, 54, 55, 57, 63, 136
Uttley, Alison 46

Valéry, Paul 11, 116
Vargas Llosa, Mario 59, 71
Varman, Anatoly 44
Verlaine, Paul 200
Vidal, Gore 43, 49, 57, 59, 61, 73, 138, 144, 146, 244
Vishniac, Roman 165
Voltaire 51, 144, 151, 201, 208, 221, 223

Wain, John 22, 24
Wainwright, A. 211
Walker, Alice 41
Walpole, Horace 138
Walton, Izaak 200
Warner, Charles Dudley 207
Warner, Jack 225
Waugh, Auberon 124, 127
Waugh, Evelyn 93

Weldon, Fay 37, 81, 83
Wellington, Duke of 150, 221
Wesker, Arnold 179
West, Mae 165
West, Rebecca 133
Wheen, Francis 62, 109
Whitehorn, Katharine 238
Wiesel, Elie 54, 131, 133, 140, 166, 168, 234, 243, 248
Wilde, Oscar 57, 91, 113, 132, 141, 175, 210, 214, 229
William Henry, Duke of Gloucester 60
Williams, Tennessee 152
Wilson, A. N. 137
Wilson, Angus 115, 190, 245
Wilson, Colin 101
Wilson, Paul 226
Winterson, Jeanette 73, 112
Wittgenstein 204
Wodehouse, P. G. 157
Wolfe, Tom 123
Woolf, Leonard 49, 74
Woolf, Virginia 21, 50, 53, 66, 67, 76, 128, 132, 135, 149, 150, 218, 223,227
Wordsworth, William 174, 238

Yeats, W. B. 214, 241
Yohai, Rabbi Simeon bar 241
Yosi, Rabbi 225
Yudkin, Leon 105